BECOMING
Love™

Nicola van Dyke

CONTENTS

Acknowledgements 3

Section 1—What is Becoming Love? ™
An Introduction to Becoming Love™ 7
Chapter 1   How to use this Book and What you can
            Expect from Working Through it 15
Chapter 2   What is the Feeling of Love we are
            Working Towards? 43

Section 2—How Do You Become Love?
Chapter 3   Reverence 59
Chapter 4   How to Be Yourself and Love Yourself 92
Chapter 5   Delving into the Heart and Soul 136
Chapter 6   Learning Love from Others 149

Section 3—Living and Becoming Love™
Chapter 7   Becoming Love™ in Practice 161
Chapter 8   Living and Becoming Love™ 175
Chapter 9   How Do You Know When You Are
            Becoming Love™? 183
Chapter 10 Are you ready? 189

Useful Information 195
About the Author 197

ACKNOWLEDGEMENTS

The idea for this book came first as a name, followed by a few flashes of inspirations over the next few months. The scribbled notes became a seminar, then a book and is now my first Creative Initiative. Becoming Love™ is my lifestyle choice and you can learn more about it through this book, the audio album, a mentoring programme, a radio show, an online learning experience and wisdom cards.

There are so many people who have influenced me, supported me, and inspired me during the creation of Becoming Love™ and you know who you are, so thank you from the bottom of my heart.

In particular I would like to thank Vianna Stibal without whom I would never have made the life changes that I have. To all my dearest friends, thank you for your support and love. To my children and my family, who have helped me practically and emotionally, my deepest gratitude.

We are all connected to every aspect of the universe and to each other as network of humanity. The ideas for Becoming Love™ came to me over time but I truly feel that they are not mine but more a collection of influences. We pick up ideas and gain experiences, from the moment we are born and our brains interpret these as our own thoughts. Becoming Love™ was already in existence in the landscape, in the whispering of the trees, in the hearts of animals, in the faces of every person and in our souls. I am honoured and grateful to have the opportunity to return it to you.

Download the Becoming Love™ Meditation Album

1. Online, visit the website www.nicolavandyke.com

2. Follow the instructions from the home page to the Becoming Love ™ album download page.

3. Follow the instructions to input your email and the following download code: **MY25364957-3645**

4. You can then use the album which has been downloaded to your device.

The album is also available to listen to on Soundcloud via the link: https://soundcloud.com/user-530532855/sets/becoming-love-meditation-1/s-rJ7Jp

SECTION 1

What is Becoming Love? ™

'I see you. I see where you stand and I love you.'
Nicola van Dyke

AN INTRODUCTION TO BECOMING LOVE™

I love you. I love that you bought or borrowed or found, or were given this book and you've opened it. I love that you are interested in finding out a little more and I am interested in *you*. I am here. Thank you.

So, what is this book about? My book is about love. Read on a little more – it's not what you think – I think! Everyone knows the phrase, 'Love makes the world go around!' It is true, in a way, for most of us, but the concept of love is a huge many faceted diamond of a word. It is the jewel of all words. It is so full of sub-meaning with pure unconditional love at its core, that the word itself is like a crystal with many points coming from its root going out in all directions. Just as all of the points make up the entire beauty of the crystal, so do all the ways in which we can show love for each other make up the beautiful energy of love.

In the English language, we only have one word for this many faceted emotion. We use the word *love* to cover a myriad of meanings, hundreds of situations, thousands of relationships, intricate nuances, varying social interactions and a cacophony of phrases. So, to clarify, this book is about a deep reverent love for yourself and for humanity. Some may use the word *agape* to describe it. This is the Greek term to describe a type of unconditional and reflective love, in which the one giving the love considers only the good of the loved one. Some Greek philosophers of Plato's time used the term to refer to universal love which could be understood as the love of truth or humanity. This book is about the feeling of love that is the desire to go on loving regardless of a response.

Becoming Love™ will support you in finding this feeling for yourself, your family, your friends and your community. It is a step by step guide to supporting you in finding this feeling of love for humanity. We are in this world together and if we can begin to find this love for each other then we can change ourselves and the network of humanity. We can change the energy of the world!

The essence of agape love is goodwill, benevolence, and the will to go on loving. It is neither romantic, sentimental nor brotherly love. The love that is agape involves faithfulness, commitment, and an act of the will. From a religious standpoint, agape is used to describe the love that is of and from God, whose very nature is love itself. Traditionally, agape is also used to describe a love for God. It is assumed that God does not merely love; He is love itself. Everything God does, flows from His love. God loves because that is the expression of His being. He loves the unlovable and the unlovely, not because we deserve to be loved or because of any excellence we possess, but because it is His nature to love and He must be true to His nature. Agape love is always shown by what it does, how it behaves, how it reacts; it just is. This is the feeling of love that you are working with in this book; an unconditional, non-romantic love for yourself and for others.

However, this is not a religious book and it is not about religion or God. You do not consciously have to believe in God or gods. I work with people every day all over the world and every single one of them has a belief in something bigger than themselves. They recognise that they, their thoughts, their successes, and their actions as an individual are not operating in a vacuum. John Donne, a seventeenth century author famously said in one of his sermons, that, 'No man is an island.' Whatever that concept means to you, whether you are religious or spiritual or have a recognition that we are sharing this planet with billions of other humans and so we are all affected by, or affect others, you will have a belief in something bigger than yourself. I wouldn't describe myself as religious although I am interested in religions from a theoretical standpoint. I wouldn't even describe myself as spiritual here in the UK where I live, because in Britain there is a general conscious belief of what a 'spiritual person' is like, and I don't resonate with its current interpretation.

However, I do believe in something bigger than myself as an individual. I am happy to call that bigger aspect, Creator. I feel this bigger aspect is within me and around me; and it feels like a loving energy. I see it in the beauty of our planet, in the loving actions of others and feel it within myself as a wisdom or a knowing. I may refer to Creator in this book to explain something and you must feel free to substitute that word for whatever works for you. Many of my clients and students use words or phrases such as the universe, Chi, the highest energy, the network of humanity, the combined human spirit, divine wisdom, God, Spirit, Source or natural energy. Use whatever word feels right for you; there is no right word except the one you feel works for you. This bigger aspect is within us and we can access it whenever we choose. We are all a drop in the ocean of this bigger aspect. Just allow yourself to fall into the unconditional ocean of love that is there for you and part of you.

My aim is that Becoming Love™ will show you how to love yourself and each other. It will support you in loving all the other humans that we share this amazing planet with; those we know and those we don't, those we meet and those we never will. My aim is to show others how to love humanity itself. Becoming Love™ is about experiencing reverence for every human being on this beautiful planet of ours.

Through reverence, treating everyone with deep respect, accepting them and cherishing them, we can change not only ourselves but, more importantly, the planet. Isn't that what we all want? Haven't you at some time thought that if only something would change, then the world would be a better place? If we had 100 people every day showing others love in their day to day lives, helping another person in a small way somewhere in the world, imagine what 1000 people in every country doing this every day could do! You can make a difference to yourself and others by one small act of love a day. What if you did two small acts of love a day? What if all of us did? *You* can change the vibration of love for all of us, in small everyday acts.

The idea for this book came to me first as a name, Becoming Love™; I didn't realise it until I noticed I had begun to use the phrase when signing off emails or referring to it on some of my Facebook posts. On noticing that I was writing it down, I began to wonder what that really meant. How could we love with reverence, unconditionally without expecting or requiring a response? The notion to put some thoughts down on paper for others began as a twinkle of inspiration, and ideas came to me over a few years, which I scribbled down on pieces of paper until I felt compelled to formulate this book.

From a child I had always known I had to be 'good' and do 'the right thing'. I learnt to keep anger and disappointments in, never to voice them so I would not be seen as moaning, complaining or disruptive. Nobody instilled this in me, I just thought that was the best way to be – it is not, by the way! I have changed and evolved so much through my life. If someone had told me ten years ago that I would have my own business with a worldwide client base, be teaching seminars, be an author, a radio presenter and intuitive mentor, I would never have believed them. I am analytical by nature and it has taken me many years to allow my intuitive, creative side to work in harmony with my logical side. My journey has been a relatively slow awakening. This book is a culmination of my experiences and work, channelled ideas and research so far, driven by my purpose.

I realise now looking back that, in my life, I unconsciously created my own problems in order to learn more about love for humanity, because this is what I came here to do. I came here to learn and to show others about it. Of course, I had some of my own learning to do first – and without doubt, I am still learning. Sometimes the greatest events push us forward and sometimes it is ongoing, seemingly small irritations from which we learn the most. Did I create situations and react in certain ways so that I obligated people and situations to teach me? Or is there a network of mutual helpers who step forward at the right time to create the situation from which we all learn? It is probably both, but which ever, I feel it is important to learn, give gratitude for the learning, lift resentments, forgive and move on with more love at your fingertips.

Through repeating experiences, I discovered that I had belief programmes running such as, *'The more challenges I overcome, the faster I grow and learn'*. Hmmm… you can imagine how that one panned out! It took me to be teaching a seminar in a foreign country, where at the last minute I found myself without a translator or materials for the seminar, to realise something was afoot! Strangely I was not stressed about the situation the night before when I realised my predicament. Rather I used my intuition, sought and found a great solution, which turned the whole seminar into a fun filled week full of unexpected joy and laughter. It was only afterwards that I thought about how my oddly calm reaction could be an indication that I was unconsciously creating unnecessary drama for a reason. I have now worked that one out of my system – I am more than happy to learn quickly and joyfully without these dramatic challenges to solve!

The more I began to create this book, the more I felt the need to become love and shine every day. I uncovered more and more beliefs systems and programmes which seemed to be helping me on my way but were also blocking me in other ways. I know it is possible to learn in an easier way! Once I discovered and released what was holding me back, I could feel the flow of the universe supporting me, and that is the feeling I would like for you to get from this book.

We can't change others, but we can change the way we behave and the way we interact with and react to others, and this in turn creates changes around us. This is not a feeling of superiority or a *'Look at me and how super enlightened I am!'* attitude. I am talking about recognising within yourself what you are creating and why, what is upsetting you and why, and so on. Don't be discouraged with what you find out about yourself, work on it, dig deep, learn to love, accept and forgive yourself. Learn to stand in your own power with the energy of *'Here I stand, I see you. I see where you stand, and I love you.'*

This is not about you having to save the world, which is an exhausting programme by the way. This book is about loving humanity, which may also include you taking some action in a variety of ways, but without obligation. The energy of *'have to'* is more comfortable when changed to *'choose to'*; it doesn't mean you will stop helping people, stop loving or stop supporting them, it just changes the energy from one of obligation to one of choice. You create your life, you have a choice, you choose.

Are you ready to Become Love?

CHAPTER 1

How to use this Book and What you can Expect from Working Through it.

Start at the beginning! I will guide you step by step to Becoming Love™. Each chapter will inspire you and invite you to question your thought patterns and behaviours. You are already perfect just as you are; a perfect work in progress. Following these steps will reveal more to you about yourself and how to love yourself and others, which will bring you peace, happiness, more joy and satisfaction.

Each step will include information, exercises for you to complete and audio meditations for you to listen to from the album, **Becoming Love™, 11 Meditations to bring you peace, happiness and joy!** The whole process of reading the book, completing the exercises and listening to the meditations will assist you on your journey. The instructions for downloading your copy of the **Becoming Love™ Meditation Album** are printed in the front and in the back of this book.

There are dedicated spaces in your book to write down your experiences and thoughts, but some people prefer to have a separate note book so they can repeat exercises. The more you use this book as a working document the more you will get out of it. If it were my copy, it would be dog eared, stuffed full of extra pieces of paper, filled in with various coloured pens, have scribbles in the margin and doodles around the edges. But if that sounds completely off putting to you, please know you can use this book and fill it out, however you choose to. Love it and make it yours. You can listen to these audio meditations on the **Becoming Love™ Meditation Album** over and over again, and each time you will gain a new experience. You can revisit any chapters, exercise or meditation as many times as you wish and I encourage you to do so. Some of the exercises will ask you to think about some statements which may reflect what you feel or would like to feel. In some chapters, you will read about the limitations of some belief programmes and you will be able to check to see if you hold any of them.

Beliefs and Programmes

We all hold thousands of programmes and beliefs on a conscious and a subconscious level. Beliefs which propel us forward and some which keep us stuck. All of us hold beliefs that we have picked up over the course of our lifetimes. We learn them from our experiences, from other people, from what we read, see, hear, and from our own actions. How we process this information from our lives and then form beliefs systems from what we witness and experience, depends on our character.

Imagine this example: A mother tells her three daughters constantly that they are all useless and will never amount to anything. Imagine her instilling in them that they should just accept that they will get pregnant and marry a useless layabout of a husband who will treat them badly. They will be stuck in the small town that they have grown up in with no money, prospects or opportunities for all of their boring, miserable lives, because they are all so stupid and worthless.

Despite the mother's words and behaviour this does not mean that all three daughters will take this information on as true and never dare to dream or take little action to improve their lives. One of the daughters may hear these words and be so outraged and insulted that she uses this anger as motivation to be highly successful. Fuelled with outrage, she may actively carve out a career for herself, move where she chooses to, and have the kind of family life she wants to, just to 'prove her mother wrong.' Another daughter may hear her mother's words and truly believe that she has no skills or options and that she is stupid. But then in her teens, she may be inspired by the words and actions of a teacher. This motivating teacher may show her that there are possibilities in the world for her and she has the ability to take them and create a great life for herself. So, she may be inspired and motivated, realise her potential, and go on to have a wonderfully happy and fulfilled life. Perhaps only one of these girls really internalises her mother's words and feels she is worthless and unable to create a different life from the one suggested by her mother. Maybe only one of these three little girls will grow into a despondent adult and have an unhappy life.

From this example it is apparent that the way we process what we learn, and develop programmes from the beliefs, depends on our own personality and other experiences. This then dictates how we as individuals behave, what we say, how we react and what actions we take in any given situation. Many of the beliefs and programmes we hold affect us in a positive, healthy way and the more you Become Love, the more you will acquire more of these.

Some beliefs we have may contradict each other. For example, if a man believed it was important to love others and wanted to, but also believed love made him vulnerable, he may have a hard time really allowing himself to commit fully to loving another, for fear of being, or being seen as, weak. Other beliefs we hold may affect us negatively, such as the last daughter in our example who believed what her mother told her and allowed this belief about herself to shape her future.

In some chapters when you are asked to consider some beliefs or programmes that you may be holding onto which are preventing you from fully Becoming Love™, you will be invited to 'test yourself' to see if you do hold them. Different therapists regularly use many accepted ways of testing for conscious or unconscious beliefs held by their clients. The one I use most frequently and find most accurate with my clients and students is this:

How to muscle test for a belief or programme

- Stand up, arms by your side, legs together, with your eyes closed, and relax. Know that there is no right or wrong response, that there is no better or worse response and that you are merely trying to discover if on some level you hold a belief programme.

- Keep your feet still and say YES aloud. Allow your body to lean; it should lean forwards. Repeat saying the word NO, and note, you should lean backwards. This may take a bit of practice. Ensure you are hydrated and allow yourself to relax; your head does not need to control this; your body knows what to do.

- Once you have got the hang of this and you are accurately testing, then say the belief you wish to check for, remembering to keep your eyes closed and to speak aloud. Allow your body to lean wherever it chooses to. If you go forward, your subconscious is indicating, YES, you do hold that belief. If you lean backwards, your subconscious is indicating, NO, you do not hold that belief.

- If you wobble about or go around in circles then it could be that on some level you do hold this belief programme but part of you does not believe it – I call these dual beliefs. They usually shift pretty easily; so, mark it down but know it will probably change as you are working and practising the ideas in this book.

- If you do not move at all, you may be dehydrated or not allowing yourself to relax into the process. There is no need to control this; just be.

- Remember whether you do or do not test positively for a belief, there is to be no self-criticism or judgement of yourself. It doesn't mean it is 'true'; it is just a belief that you hold. It is something to note and it can be changed so you can Become Love with more ease and joy. There is no point in trying to the 'cheat the system' as the only person who is going to lose out is you; if you do not know what you need to work on to find more love and happiness in your life, how can you hope to achieve it?

If you do hold some of the beliefs and programmes which may be holding you back from Becoming Love™, do not worry! By reading and working through this book, listening to the meditations, and taking the actions suggested, you may well find that when you re-test, your limiting belief programmes have changed. You may want to work on root issues, clear them faster or you may find that despite your commitment to the ideas within this book, you still hold some of the beliefs programmes. If so, you could choose to work with a professional to clear them, so you can move forward more joyfully and easily. There are a number of ways you can do this.

In my work as a mentor supporting people worldwide to make changes to their lives, I specialise in the ThetaHealing® technique. I am committed to assisting you in being your authentic self and loving your life; in being true to yourself and loving yourself. I am passionate about showing people how to love each other; I believe that this is easier when you love yourself and feel how you belong in the universe. I assist people in taking steps to being successful, feeling happiness, having abundance and living in love by changing limiting belief programmes.

I use this cutting-edge holistic modality which is both a meditation technique and a spiritual philosophy. It is a training method for your mind, body and spirit that allows you to clear limiting beliefs and live life with positive thoughts whilst developing virtues. It is always to be used in conjunction with conventional medicine. If you are interested in finding out more about how I work with clients, you can visit my website and, in the back of this book, there are several internet links that you may find useful if you want to find out more about the entire Becoming Love™ creative initiative, the work that I do or the ThetaHealing® technique. Of course, there are other therapies or modalities that can assist you in changing limiting belief programmes within levels of your conscious and subconscious, such as NLP, CBT, hypnosis and EFT. If you do seek professional help, my advice is to choose whichever method you feel comfortable with and ensure you find a practitioner that you trust.

Becoming Love™ Meditations

Each of the guided meditations on the **Becoming Love™ Meditation Album** are different and you will be advised when it is most relevant to listen to each one as you go through the book. This doesn't mean you can only listen to them then. You can listen to them whenever you like. Before listening to each track, you will need to find a quiet place where you can relax undisturbed for about half an hour. Each time you will hear my voice guiding you into a deep state of meditation.

When we quieten our minds into the relaxed state that I use when I am meditating, in scientific terms we are achieving a theta brainwave. (*In human EEG studies, the term 'theta' refers to frequency components in the 4–7 Hz range, regardless of their source. Cortical theta is observed frequently in young children. ["Cortical theta rhythms" are low-frequency components of scalp EEG, usually recorded from humans.] In older children and adults, it tends to appear during meditative, drowsy, hypnotic or sleeping states. (Wikipedia 1/18)*). Many babies and young children under the age of 7 are in a theta brainwave for much of the time. As we grow up, we achieve this deep theta brainwave naturally at least twice a day, just as we drop off to sleep and when we first wake up. We can also 'train' our minds to go into this state when we meditate. The method I use to guide you into this lovely meditative state, the theta brainwave, on every meditation on the **Becoming Love™ Meditation Album,** uses the 'road map' created by Vianna Stibal and is described in her book ThetaHealing®.

When you listen to my words or read the 'road map', it implies we are going up or out of our bodies, and travelling somewhere out beyond the universe. Of course, in reality, we are not really going anywhere. The words describe going up out of our heads and up out of the universe through layers of lights; or expanding out into and past the universe and layers of light, into a sparkly, white light. However, this is just a route to reference, in order to teach us the technique to slow our brain down when we choose to. When we practise the 'road map', we are merely training our brains to go into this slower, theta state and, once we have a good muscle memory, we can achieve this state without following the words but by just doing it.

During meditations we are not really going anywhere. All we have is within us already. We have divine wisdom within us and so we have our own answers. We can be our own support, guidance and wisdom because by achieving a theta brainwave we are accessing the more intuitive parts of our brain; our minds are more able to conceive of the infinite possibilities of the universe in a theta brainwave. Many inventors and creatives such as musicians and artists will say they get their best ideas when they wake up first thing in the morning, perhaps as if they dreamed it. Our brain is an amazing organ and, when it is in a theta state, it is highly intuitive, creative and wise.

When you are in this brain wave, it is much easier to allow yourself to recognise that love is flowing through you all the time and that allows you to shine loving energy out to everyone you meet. Your aim is to take this feeling into your daily life; to allow it to spill into your day to day living experience. The more you listen to the meditations, the more easily you will soon you be able to train your brain to slip into this highly intuitive state. The more you practise the easier it is.

Ready to Start?

This is not a one-stop self-help book. It is a learning system full of information to support you, exercises to get you thinking, and meditations to assist you in finding a more loving state of being. It is not a quick fix for your life. It is a guide to Becoming Love™ which is a lifestyle choice. The more you allow yourself to experience even small changes to the way you think and behave, the easier you will find your everyday life, as well as making changes to others' lives too. I really believe that the vibration of love can change the world!

You are an amazing, beautiful, unique person and I want you to feel loved and supported by yourself, others in your life, others who are working to Becoming Love™ and by me. We humans are a team and you are never alone. The Becoming Love™ community forum is there for you to access further information and continued updates. It is a safe space to ask questions, read and share inspirational messages and stories, and to get support from me and each other. There is an online programme you can join which assists you with all the information and exercises in this book as well as offering one to one sessions. Through the online programme you can access webinars and the meditations, so you can enjoy continuous guidance and encouragement on your journey to Becoming Love™.

Welcome to Becoming Love™!

My Wish for You

I am motivated by love and by my desire to teach others about loving reverence. What would happen if all of us in this city or this county, or this world, could attain new virtues and be free of negative beliefs? How would all our new feelings and behaviour, all this love, change the world and humanity? Through my work as a life mentor, I witness changes in myself and others every day. I see the difference positive beliefs, attitudes and behaviour make to our lives. I support people in changing negative beliefs which are holding them back or creating negative patterns of behaviour, so they can live the life they want to and feel the way they want to. The more they feel positive thoughts such as patience, determination, happiness, love, faith, kindness, empathy, joy, integrity and sympathy etc., the more their life changes.

I like to think that if you have enough virtues it would be possible to heal by touch. As a professional mentor and healer, this is my 'God dream'. However, I want to take it one step further! My biggest dream is to stand and have others who come near me feel healed, and then their healing allows others to heal, so in a matter of time everyone on earth is healed and a healer, through love itself. Ancient prophets said that the more humans attain virtues, the quicker they would help rid the planet of vices. It has to be worth a go!

Making the world a better place is wonderful, but what will *you* get from reading this book, completing the exercises and listening to the meditations? The Becoming Love™ creative initiative aims to teach you to feel love for yourself so you can also feel love for humanity. Love begets love. This is the beginning. You are all reading this to achieve different things, you are all at different points in your life and have had different experiences. This book is part of your journey into Becoming Love™, and afterwards you will have more skills and techniques with which to continue on your path and to help others do so too, if you choose to.

Why Become Love?

Before we begin to really explore some profound ways in which you can Become Love, would you like to understand why it is so important to you and to all of us? Simply speaking, love is the strongest emotion on the planet!

> *'Whenever I get gloomy with the state of the world, I think about the arrivals gate at Heathrow Airport. General opinion's starting to make out that we live in a world of hatred and greed, but I don't see that. It seems to me that love is everywhere. Often, it's not particularly dignified or newsworthy, but it's always there - fathers and sons, mothers and daughters, husbands and wives, boyfriends, girlfriends, old friends. When the planes hit the Twin Towers, as far as I know, none of the phone calls from the people on board were messages of hate or revenge - they were all messages of love. If you look for it, I've got a sneaky feeling you'll find that love actually is all around.'*
> The Prime Minister words from the film, Love Actually 2003

Love truly *is* the strongest emotion on the planet and this is the primary reason for reading and working through this book. Love is strength. With this love and with this strength, we can change the planet. Isn't that what we all want to do in some way? Our collective consciousness to make this world a better, healthier place is bigger than ourselves and our own needs. It is bigger than the needs of our family. We can do wonderful things for many people on our wonderful planet through love.

The following exercise is something I did quite by accident the first time and I now consciously do on a weekly basis. It allows you to really see the love that there is out there in the world, which is happening every day everywhere, without anyone really noticing. It is a beautiful exercise because it opens your heart to really seeing the potential in humanity and in yourself, and it is through this realisation that you understand why Becoming Love™ is so nourishing for you and for others.

Exercise: *Catch them being good!*

Pick a journey! Choose any simple every day or any day journey, like going to work or going to the supermarket. On that journey, I want you to really open your eyes and notice what is going on as you travel. I did this experiment one morning on my way to my work and on that morning, I saw:

- A young woman helping a mother off the bus with her cumbersome pushchair.

- A school crossing lollipop man wiping away a boy's tears after he fell over.

- A shopkeeper taking a few pennies less than the price of some teabags from an old lady.

- Strangers stopping to chat and smile as their dogs connected on the street.

- A driver at a busy junction waving other drivers through with a cheery smile.

- A neighbour snipping another's overgrown hedge as they are too frail to do it themselves.

- A man stopping to hold open the huge street bin lid for a child who was trying to drop their litter into it.

This what is what I saw on my walk to work and it's a short walk! In less than five minutes I saw all of these wonderful people doing wonderful random acts of humanity. What can *you* experience when you catch us all being good one day, on one of your short journeys somewhere?

You can write down what you observed in the space below and don't be surprised if there isn't enough room for all of the things you saw. Try doing this on a regular basis and notice how it makes you feel good. You will feel good about yourself and your place in the world.

Nicola van Dyke

On my journey, I saw.......

Benefits of Becoming Love™

I love people! There is nothing new in what we are talking about here. People have been encouraging others to have reverence for each other for thousands of years, inspiring us all to act and react with love. Every religion and many philosophies about humanity over the centuries have the same messages about love:

- Love others.

- Treat others as you would like to be treated.

- Show respect for all.

There must be some truth in the necessity for it and benefits of it, if everyone has been saying it all over the world for so long! When you feel love for yourself and others you will feel happier, more relaxed and yet more energised in your day to day life. There are also more benefits.

3 More Great Reasons to Become Love

1. In order to create what you want to have in your life, you can do it more easily if you have the virtue of love. You can't manifest, that is, create the life you wish for, if you don't consider yourself worthy and deserving, if you don't love yourself or have good intentions. You are accountable for building and creating your life. Taking responsibility for that design requires self-love and love for others, in terms of respect, reverence and acceptance.

2. The more you clear any resentments you hold towards yourself and others in order to Become Love, the lighter you feel and possibly become. This really can be

physically too! Health experts have proved that toxins in our cells can cause you to retain physical weight. Negative emotions such as resentment, hatred and anger are toxic to our body. By reading and working through this book, you will naturally and effortlessly begin to release these negative emotions that you have been holding onto. You will definitely feel lighter and more relaxed. As you release toxins both physical and energetically by releasing the negative emotions, your cells can release fat that has been trapped by the toxins and you just might drop a few kilos too!

3. Love, so you can move forward. If you are full of fear, anger, feelings of revenge and hatred, you are moving backwards. However, the more you love the more you move forward. Consider this on a physical level. Bruce H. Lipton, PhD, author of, *The Biology of Belief*, explains this concept clearly. If you put a human cell in a petri dish with a toxic compound, it will move away from it. If you put a human cell in a petri dish with a form of nutrition it will move towards it. Each of us is just a huge collection of human cells. When you see someone you love on the street, you move towards them quickly to hug them, and to talk to them. I expect that if you saw a lion chasing shoppers in a busy mall you would turn and run away in fear. If you saw a person you disliked you might turn off down a side street to avoid a confrontation. We as humans react to love the same way as we do to nutrition, we move forward. We react to fear and hate in the same way as we react to toxins, we move backwards. You cannot move both backwards and forwards at the same time. So, we need love to move forward. We need to feel loved and to love without fear, hatred or anger. We can move forward as individuals

in love when we clear our own negativity and we can move forward as a network of humanity in love when we work on our jealousy and fear. In life, do you want to move forward or backwards? I know which direction I choose to move in!

I invite you to love! Love, in order to move forward, feel lighter, create the life you want and have respect for all, including yourself!

> *'Love and compassion are necessities, not luxuries. Without them humanity cannot survive.'*
> Dalai Lama

Let's Make a Start!

I have always felt that I wanted to live a life of purpose, to accomplish something; I just didn't know what that was. My life journey has taught me that part of that purpose is to encourage others to feel agape and reverence for humanity. My purpose is bigger than me, it allows me to be bigger than myself, and is pushing me to be the best version of me I can be. It is through living my purpose that I am reminded every day to revere the life on our planet. You only have to look into a person or an animal's eyes to be reminded that life is the essence of our existence on this planet, and how love keeps that life alive. The exercise below is to allow you to experience this wholeheartedly for a few weeks; or as long as you choose!

> *'A loving heart, a heart full of love, is the precious essence of human life.'*
> Maharishi Mahesh Yogi (from Love and God)

Exercise: *Where there is Love, there is Life*

You may have heard of the self-love mirror exercise developed by Louise Hay. This exercise, *Where There is Love, there is Life*, builds on that concept.

1. Every day for the next week, perhaps when you are brushing your teeth, look at your face in the mirror. Look deeply into your own eyes for about 30 seconds. Notice how you feel and what thoughts cross your mind. Then say 'I love you.'

2. Each time write a quick note of how you felt doing this. For the first week you will probably feel pretty silly, by the second week you may find you start to notice all the things about your face, or your body or yourself that you don't like. You will notice your wrinkles, pimples and blemishes, your loose flesh, lumps and bony bits - but you are going to do it and say it anyway. By the third week you will feel a wonderful warm feeling coming over you when you look deeply into your own eyes. That is the beginning of self-love.

3. Also, every day over these three weeks I want you to start looking into other people's eyes. Really look at them. Notice the essence of them, and in just a second, feel their humanity. Now you know you have to be careful to whom you do this! Perhaps try it with your family first. Your librarian or co-worker may feel a little uncomfortable under such intense scrutiny!

4. The next step, if and when you feel comfortable, is to choose people whom you already have a close relationship with, and when you look deep into their eyes, say

'I love you.' You are not saying this in a romantic way, not just because they are your child or your sibling, but as a fellow human being.

5. Make a few notes on how you felt and what you experienced over the course of the three weeks. You will notice how the feeling of being very uncomfortable looking deep into someone's eyes for a moment or two, soon becomes second nature, and you will realise the value of that human connection in all your interactions. Of course, you are not going to say 'I love you' to many people, but the gentle yet profound eye contact with most people is a great social interaction to work towards. You will feel your connection to them and to humanity as a whole.

You will be doing this daily exercise for a few weeks and there is space for you to make some notes of your experiences below, but carry straight on with the rest of this book whilst you take a minute every day to do the exercise.

Nicola van Dyke

Exercise: *My Experiences of Where There is Love There is Life*

Day	Looking into my own eyes I experienced...	Looking into someone else's eyes, I experienced...
1		
2		
3		
4		
5		
6		
7		

Day	Looking into my own eyes I experienced...	Looking into someone else's eyes, I experienced...
8		
9		
10		
11		
12		
13		
14		

Day	Looking into my own eyes I experienced…	Looking into someone else's eyes, I experienced…
15		
16		
17		
18		
19		
20		
21		

> *'Where there is love there is life.'*
> Mahatma Ghandi

We are all life, so we are all capable of love. I believe it is the shared purpose of many of us to evolve the planet through love, one person at a time. That doesn't mean we don't all have our own individual purposes too. None of us operate in isolation however, and our purpose affects everyone else in our life, in the community and for some of us, in the world. We are all uniquely wonderful individuals, who make up a network of humanity.

Many life coaches will tell you that whatever your passion is, it is probably linked to your purpose and the sooner you realise this, the quicker things fall into place for you. My passion is humanity; my passion is you. I love people and I love you. My passion is agape for humanity and for you. My purpose is to tell you all about it and how you can spread light throughout the world by loving yourself and humanity; how to do it, why it is so cool, and how to keep on doing it in your everyday life. You don't have to wait to be perfectly good or full of virtuous intention to do this, you are already ready. You are a spark of love in this universe; let the feeling of love shine into you and through you, and your love for others will show.

Some people do this naturally. They seem to be born with the energy of sunshine, shining love and happiness to others without even trying; they just do it every day. These sunny people pick up on a lack of love in situations in a blink of an eye and are able to shine brighter. Many small children have this quality, but as they grow older sometimes life gets in the way and they forget how to be so shiny. A young girl I know was invited to stay at a relative's house a few years ago. The family are financially abundant and have a beautiful home with a large garden, a tennis court, a pool, stables and a number of 'staff'. After her trip I asked her how her holiday had been, expecting an enthusiastic response. Instead she said, *'There was lots to do and I was never bored but it's kind of all <u>wrong</u> there. At their home, they have everything most people would say they wanted. They have more cars than adults who can drive, a huge cinema TV, an organic vegetable patch tended by a gardener, more sitting rooms than people in the house, and ...... everything!! But they are not happy and they think they don't have enough things. They buy more and more things but they don't realise that they will never be happy because the thing they don't have is love. I don't just mean the mummy and daddy. They don't show love at all; not for the children, nor for the people who come to the house to help them, nor for people they meet out and about. They just don't get it - but that's okay; they will learn.'* It didn't faze her, she didn't feel it was her job to fix them, and she didn't take on their unhappiness. She just noticed and continued to shine, and to carry on loving. She knows that love is contagious! I have learnt a lot from this little girl; we can all learn a lot from each other! Are you ready? Do want to learn how to shine?

What would happen if you could love everyone without judgement? Love without fear, anger or hatred? Love without having to defend yourself, be betrayed or being jealous? What would it feel like to love without feeling criticised, attacked, comparing yourself to others or thinking negatively? Can you imagine the freedom of being able to love someone without feeling that you have to fix them or change them? Would you like to know what that feels like and how to achieve this?

Feeling Your Way to Love

As amazing souls in human form, we have feelings. We learn them over our life time from our experiences, other people and the social consciousness, and develop them according to our personality. Many of us, due to 'incorrect' information, learn a feeling in a different way to what that feeling really is. For example, imagine a child who is constantly reprimanded or abused by a parent who tells them *'I am only doing this because I love you.'* That child will learn in their formative years that love comes hand in hand with criticism and pain. As they grow up, when they are showing and receiving love from others, they may be seeking or delivering this kind of love because that is what they have learnt love is. Obviously how we learn and what we do with that learning is dependent on our own personality and other experiences, but on a very simplistic level this example illustrates how all of us can interpret a feeling in a less than desirable way. Furthermore, some of us never learn certain feelings at all, depending on our life to date. What if you had never experienced joy or love in your life to date?

The next exercise is designed to assist you in acquiring certain feelings which will help you to Become Love. Firstly, take a pen and read the statements of feelings below. Circle YES to any of them that you would like to feel or think you already do feel. The second part of this exercise is a meditation, **Feeling Your Way to Love**, *track 1*, on the **Becoming Love™ Meditation Album**. Having done this quick written exercise, you will make yourself comfortable and listen to the first meditation on the album.

Exercise: *Feeling your way to Love* 1

Feelings you may have or wish to have.	Circle the word YES if you would like to have this feeling or feel you already do have it.
Would you like to already know and understand what agape (love) is?	YES
Would you like to already know how to feel agape (love) for humanity in your day to day life?	YES
Would you like to already know and understand what reverence is?	YES
Would you like to already know how to feel reverence for humanity in your day to life?	YES
Would you like to already know how to feel this love for humanity in your day to day life without…?	
Anger?	YES
Hatred?	YES
Judgement?	YES
Criticism?	YES
Feeling depressed?	YES
Feeling or being inferior?	YES
Feeling or being superior?	YES

Being or feeling belittled?	YES
Being or feeling persecuted?	YES
Being or feeling betrayed?	YES
Being or feeling attacked?	YES
Being or feeling defeated?	YES
Being or feeling overwhelmed?	YES
Being or feeling judged?	YES
Being or feeling discouraged?	YES
Having to provoke or provoking jealousy?	YES
Comparing yourself to others?	YES
Thinking negatively?	YES
Having to fix anyone?	YES

You will be reminded of all of these feelings and some others on the first, **Feeling Your Way to Love Meditation,** which you can listen to as many times as you like. A little further on in the book you will be invited to listen to this first meditation again, so if you prefer you can wait until then. Or you can do it now and then again later!

Meditation: *Feeling Your Way to Love*

> Make yourself comfortable in a quiet place where you will not be disturbed for about 30 minutes. You could sit or lie down. Now, listen to the **Feeling Your Way to Love Meditation** which is *track 1,* on the **Becoming Love**™ **Meditation Album.**
>
> All of the feelings in the exercise above are included on this 1st meditation; as you listen to it, you can just allow the sound of my voice to wash over you and relax. You don't need to respond if you hear me asking you a question because by completing the questions above you have already made your intentions clear, but if you choose to affirm or not in your head, you can do so. Relax and enjoy now!

CHAPTER 2

What is the Feeling of Love we are Working Towards?

What is love? It is a beautiful, rainbow coloured, crystal of a word. A word like a crystal lattice extending in all directions with many meanings. However, in English we use the same word for the emotion one may feel for a lover, or a friend, or a child, or God, or a sibling. Other languages and cultures have many words for love. In the Buddhist teaching of love there are four elements. The first is *maître* which describes friendship, brotherhood and a loving kindness. The second is *karuna*, which is a capacity to understand suffering and to help to remove and transform it; it is a similar energy to compassion. *Mudita* is the third element and it describes joy; your joy is his or her joy; his or her joy is our joy. The last element is *upeksha* which is an attitude of non-discrimination. This is a higher form of love. The four qualities have no limits, they are all infinite love. With only one word to express love as a concept, perhaps we in the English speaking world are somehow disadvantaged.

> '*Sanskrit has ninety-six words for love; ancient Persian has eighty, Greek three, and English only one. This is indicative of the poverty of awareness or emphasis that we give to that tremendously important realm of feeling. Eskimos have thirty words for snow, because it is a life-and death matter to them to have exact information about the element they live with so intimately. If we had a vocabulary of thirty words for love ... we would immediately be richer and more intelligent in this human element so close to our heart. An Eskimo probably would die of clumsiness if he had only one word for snow; we are close to dying of loneliness because we have only one word for love. Of all the Western languages, English may be the most lacking when it comes to feeling*'.
>
> Robert Johnson, *Fisher King and the Handless Maiden* 1995

Love is what it is for us native English speakers, and we tend to expect others to know what we mean when we express our love in words. It is used so commonly amongst teenage girls to their friends as to have lost all meaning and yet can be the scariest thing to say to your partner near the beginning of a relationship. Over thousands of years, poets and philosophers have tried to define what love is, scientists cannot quantify it, but it is accepted that we human beings need it, thrive on it and will move mountains for it. In whatever way we use the word, we want and need the emotion in our life. This wonderful, crystal-lattice like emotion is the strongest emotion on the planet. It encompasses all of the emotions that are in the word-mesh diagram, as well as many others. Love is all of these emotions and more!

Love has no room for anger, hypocrisy, judgement, grudges, jealousy, hatred, meanness or fear within its splendour and wonder.

All empowering love coming from you to others, and from others to you, can lead to an amazing increase in your positive emotions, abilities and skills. When you love yourself and feel loved by others, when you feel supported, motivated, inspired and encouraged positively by others and the world around you, then you can do even greater things. You feel safe to experiment, to question and to voice your imaginative ideas. Your creativity, wisdom, and inventiveness increase as you experience trust and faith in yourself, others and the world around you. You become more intuitive and peaceful, more willing and courageous to try new things and become more open to more people. Love is an amazing emotion in its complexity and effectiveness on our well-being. The aspect of love that Becoming Love™ really focusses on is *reverence*, a deep respect for another that is essential to the concept of agape. Reverence is an aspect of love for one another that is akin to a deep regard for another human being.

Imagine the complex emotion of love as a crystal. At the centre of this crystal is how I would describe the highest energy in the universe's love, for all of creation. It is the essence of unconditional love - the love that *just is*. Enveloping unconditional love is the emotion of reverence, and this feeling of reverence is essential to showing and feeling unconditional love. Reverence is sometimes considered a rather old-fashioned virtue but I believe it is key to all love and it is this feeling that is Becoming Love™.

When I imagine the emotion of love as a crystal with a central orb of unconditional love surrounded by reverence, it seems to me that all the other emotions and feelings that are also an aspect of love, grow as crystal points from this solid centre in all different directions. All of these are the emotions and the feelings we have for others in our lives as well as ourselves and they all stem from pure unconditional love and reverence. These feelings and emotions include, amongst others, respect, trust, compassion, integrity, empathy, passion, kindness, forgiveness, sympathy, acceptance, honour and care.

Reverence is the key to all of the major philosophies on love, and whilst some pay more attention to some aspects of this love than others, the message is always clear. Love in its purest form neither weakens nor diminishes you. You can maintain your boundaries with love, you can say 'No' with love and you can still allow yourself to recognise all of your human emotions with love. You can love yourself and love others.

Some virtues which are aspects of love are seen by some people as a weakness or a sign of vulnerability. Gentleness, patience, remaining calm and humility are all aspects of behaviour which we may see in others, and unconsciously seek to take advantage of. We may perceive them as weak. Alternatively, others may see these virtues in you and dismiss your needs and actions because you are not assertive or loud enough. Truly it is the perception of these virtues that we must change. In terms of interacting with others we should take care to notice each other, to make room for everyone, to allow others to shine. There is no need to push, to talk over others, to rush all the time, just to make sure *you* are noticed. You are unique. What you have to offer is unique and there is room for all of us unique beings to shine.

If you are practising gentleness, patience, being calm and humility, wonderful! But know you can be kind *and* assertive, patient *and* act promptly, remain calm *and* speak your truth and be humble *whilst* knowing and reflecting your own value. Loving virtues are strong. You can be proud of yourself without fearing you will become arrogant. You can feel and know you are good enough without having to push others out of the way. Become Love!

What is Love?

The next exercise is designed to assist you in acquiring certain feelings, which will help you to Become Love by understanding what love is. Firstly, take a pen and read the statements of feelings below. Circle YES to any of them that you would like to feel or think you already do feel. The second part of this exercise is to make yourself comfortable and listen to the first meditation on the **Becoming Love™ Meditation Album**, *Feeling Your Way to Love*. If you did already listen to this first meditation immediately after the last exercise, then you do not have to listen to this again now, but you can do.

Exercise: *Feeling Your Way to Love 2*

Feelings You Already Have or Wish to Have	Circle the word YES if you would like to have this feeling or feel you already do have it.
Would you like to already know how to and what it feels like to love yourself?	YES
Would you like to already know the power of love?	YES
Would you like to already know what it feels like to love humanity?	YES
Would you like to already know what if feels like to be love?	YES
Would you like to already know what it means to be and feels like to be, a spark of unconditional loving energy?	YES
Would you like to already know that you are love?	YES
Would you like to already know what it feels like to be strong?	YES

All of these feelings above and those from the last feeling exercise, **Feeling Your Way to Love 1**, are included on *Track 1, Feeling Your Way to Love Meditation,* on the **Becoming Love™ Meditation Album**, which you can listen to now and as many times as you like.

Meditation: *Feeling Your Way to Love*

> Make yourself comfortable in a quiet place where you will not be disturbed for about 30 minutes. You could sit or lie down. Now, listen to the ***Feeling Your Way to Love Meditation*** which is *track 1,* on the **Becoming Love™ Meditation Album.**
>
> All of the feelings in the exercise above and from the previous feelings exercise are included on this 1st meditation; as you listen to it, you can just allow the sound of my voice to wash over you and relax. You don't need to respond if you hear me asking you a question because by completing the questions above you have already made your intentions clear, but if you choose to affirm or not in your head, you can do so. Relax and enjoy now!

Programmes and Beliefs That May be Holding You Back from Becoming Love™

Below are some beliefs or programmes that you may have which could be holding you back from Becoming Love™. In the first chapter of this book, you will find some information on how to test for beliefs that you may consciously or subconsciously hold. Test the beliefs below now to see if you have any of these programmes. The desired response is written next to the programme in brackets. For example, on the first one, 'Loving others makes me weak,' the response you are hoping to get when you test yourself is 'No.'

When testing yourself, if you do have any of the limiting beliefs, you can just put a pen mark next to them. If you have the 'desired response,' do not mark them at all; they do not apply to you and you don't have to think about them.

Stand up and test the beliefs below, as you learnt in Chapter 1. Remember to ensure that you are testing YES/NO correctly, before you start, to speak aloud and have your eyes closed.

Exercise: *Limiting Belief Programmes Regarding Becoming Love™ to Check*

	Belief to Check	Desired Response	Your check mark*
1	Loving others makes me weak	No	
2	Sharing my love makes me weak	No	
3	Sharing my love makes me vulnerable	No	
4	Being able to love is a strength	Yes	
5	Being able to receive love is a strength	Yes	
6	I fear being loved	No	
7	It is safe for me to love others	Yes	
8	I am allowed to love myself	Yes	
9	I am allowed to love others	Yes	
10	It is safe for others if I love them	Yes	
11	I am allowed to love humanity	Yes	
12	If I love humanity, I can save them	No	
13	If I love humanity, I will have to save everyone	No	

If you do hold any of these potentially limiting beliefs programmes, and you will probably hold many of them, don't panic! By the time you have read this book, practised the exercises and listened to the meditations, you will already be much closer to Becoming Love™ and you will have already changed these beliefs within you. So, come back to them at the end and re-test the ones you thought you held and enjoy witnessing the transformation. (You do not need to test those you never held in the first place, just the ones you originally marked.) If after this you find you are still holding some of these beliefs or if you would like to clear them faster, there are different ways of doing this and these are discussed in chapter 1.

Aspects of Love

Over many thousands of years, philosophers, religions, gurus and leaders have offered up ideas on morality and ways to behave. They can seem complicated or difficult to apply to our modern society, or they may appear to contradict each other causing confusion; but if we aim to behave within the crystal-like emotion of love, to master as many of the facets within it as we can, whether it be compassion or forgiveness, or any of them, then we are working within love. There are so many aspects of love and we can aim to be the most loving we can be towards ourselves and others. Some aspects of love are easier to master than others and we all have aspects of love we find easy to master and others we find more difficult. Some of us are incredibly generous but find it difficult to receive. Some of us find it easy to be compassionate with others but not with ourselves. Some of us are great at self-nurturing but not so good at nurturing others. There is no better or worse way to be; the ideal is to Become Love. If we can master reverence itself then we are even closer to Becoming Love™, closer to the love that mirrors love that 'just is'. The aspect of love that many of us find the most difficult to get to grips with is forgiveness.

Forgiveness

In my work, one of the facets of love people ask me to support them with the most is forgiveness. Forgiving when others do not, or being unable to forgive, causes so much unhappiness for people. There is a secret reason why it is so hard to forgive others and it is possible to overcome it.

> *'Forgiveness is the forward action of giving love.'*
> Sean Michael Campbell

This idea of forgiveness, a forward action of giving love, sounds beautiful. It is a beautiful way to describe the power of forgiveness but it still doesn't make it easy to do. When we feel hurt or upset by another person, we hold onto the negative feelings of anger or sadness. We carry them around like a suitcase, and feel heavy and weighed down by the emotion. We remain attached to the person that has wronged us or the unbearable situation and continue to think about them or it, simply because we are carrying around this suitcase of negativity.

Why do we do that? It's heavy carrying around those dark emotions, having them flare up out of the blue to spoil our day – but we do, willingly carry them around. All over the world humans are carrying excess baggage; and some have been carrying these emotions around with them for years and years. In my work, I support people every day who have bags full of anger, sadness and hate toward someone who has wronged them. How often do you hear people tell you that they don't talk to 'so and so' since 200x, or they haven't seen their sister since they were teenagers?

These grudges, resentments and feelings of anger and hurt which we hold onto are heavy and toxic but we continue to hold onto them like precious possessions. We don't forgive. Why not?

The reason people find it so hard to forgive is fear.

The fear is that, if we do forgive, we have to allow these dark emotions to go. We will have to put down the excess baggage - and if we do that, what is it that we really fear? What is the actual fear? What is the secret reason we don't forgive?

What we really fear is *forgetting* and then being vulnerable again, allowing the other person to hurt us or let us down again. Holding onto the anger makes us feel empowered; it is like an armour protecting us from being hurt. Holding onto the painful memories is a safe way to remind us not to go near that person again, or not to put ourselves in that position again - and it works! It works really well. If you hate or resent another for the pain they put you through, you are never going to let them into your life again. All of a sudden, you are safe from them.

Or are you? How's it working out for you, feeling anger under the surface all the time?

Do you have to avoid some social occasions in case you run into them? Do you feel cross with yourself that you still feel sadness about the situation? Do you feel heavy, bitter and resentful? Do you find yourself blindsided by hatred or sorrow during the day when something reminds you of that person or what happened to you? It's not a great way to live. It actually hurts you more than them – they usually have no idea how you feel and if they do, they probably don't care – or worse, they take pleasure in your discomfort. So how safe and protected do you feel now?

If the fear of forgetting is the reason why humans find it so hard to forgive, would you like to know that it *is* possible to forgive easily without feeling or being vulnerable? The secret to being able to forgive is simple. What if were possible to be discerning, to remember who and what situations are safe for you, without holding onto anger or hatred towards anyone? What if you could move on with your life knowing how to keep yourself safe from these kinds of people and situations without carrying around parcels of grudges, or feeling dried up with bitterness?

It is possible and easy. Knowing the difference between forgetting and forgiveness is the key. Forgiveness is not forgetting. Forgiveness means you give up the pattern of continuing to blame. You still know what happened, who was involved and you have learnt to have discernment to protect yourself in the future. You don't have to consciously remember all the gory details or relive it ever again. You just need to know you have learnt anything you need to, such as who and when to trust, and that you have discernment going forward.

By forgiving you are sending love to yourself and giving yourself permission to let go. You can let go of the heavy baggage of resentments, grudges and hate. It is safe to forgive yourself and others because you have learnt discernment going forward; you won't forget to look after yourself or be more careful in the future – but the past is over and forgiven. You can move forward with a light, positive attitude. Would you like to know that you are worthy and deserving of having this understanding? Would you like to know what it feels like to forgive yourself and others? Would you like to know that is safe to, you are allowed to, you can and you do?

Now when you recall a situation where you think you have done wrong and feel shame, you can forgive yourself knowing you know better now. Or if you remember someone who has hurt you, you can forgive and detach yourself from the negativity knowing you have discernment in the future.

Forgiveness is strength. Be strong with the ability to forgive with ease and feel the love shining into you.

Can you Recognise Love all Around you?

Recognising that love is all around you is easy! Love is everywhere! The more you recognise it, the more you will see it. Have you noticed how many heart shapes appear in nature? Exactly when in history the romantic heart shape began to be used commonly to depict love is unknown, but it did start appearing in images from the middle ages. Some say it originated from the ancient use of the fig leaf which is shaped rather like a romantic heart shape and it was used much earlier in expressions of fertility. For sure, nature seems to mirror the design and you see hearts wherever you look in the shapes of leaves, petals, stones, quirky vegetables and tree hollows. The exact origin of the heart shape to depict love is lost in the mists of time, but just take a moment today to see how love is all around us every day on our beautiful planet. How many heart shapes can you find in one day in the natural environment or around your home or office?

Shapes of hearts are fun to observe but seeing the emotion is even better! It is possible to see love everywhere - in the way animal parents care for their young and your pets look at you adoringly. You see it in the synergy of the universe; how the sunshine works in harmony with the rain to produce food for the planet. Love is everywhere in nature and love is everywhere in your everyday life in simple human interactions. The more you see love for humanity between others, the easier it will be for you to love others. Of course, people do bad things – we see it on the news every day and we may experience it in our lives; but you know, on the whole, most people do good things. Every day, millions of people do simple, little acts of kindness, sharing and compassion. All you have to do is to start to notice, and the more you do, the more you will notice more, and the more your faith in humanity will be realised. Practising the Catch Them Being Good exercise from Chapter 1 always works for me when I need to be reminded of the essential good in all of us.

SECTION 2

How Do You Become Love?

'When you can feel another's heart and their truth, then loving them is easy. If you could see their soul, the essence of them, their spirit.... if you could, just for a second ... imagine what you could feel for them.'

Nicola van Dyke

CHAPTER 3

Reverence

It is widely thought that we should be more loving towards each other as a human race, but how do we do it? How do we Become Love? Actually, it is easy. It is the miracle of accepting people and loving them as they are, without having to change them, feel that we are responsible for their emotions or actions, or take on their stuff; just love them. That is reverence.

If someone is behaving badly, the issue isn't them or you specifically; it is that you are judging them for their behaviour. You can love and accept someone but you don't need to have them in your life or allow them to affect your life. You can say 'No' with love, and have boundaries with love.

Allow people to own their own emotions. I know of a family unit who all tiptoe around the father so they 'don't make him angry.' He is not physically violent but he shouts, sulks, controls and humiliates. The adult children in this family consider this normal and accept that they must 'behave' so they don't make him angry. So as adults they do not have complete control over their own lives. When one of their friends pointed out that many of his behaviours were unusual and unreasonable they could not see that; this family dynamic was normal to them. When it was suggested that they could perhaps calmly discuss their decisions and choices with their parents and if their father got angry then so be it, they were shocked – they could not handle the consequences or even imagining doing or saying anything that might 'make Dad angry'. They all believe that they are responsible for their father's emotions; that if he gets angry it is their fault.

In this context, by taking on responsibility for another's emotions you are in effect disempowering them. You are never allowing them to take responsibility for their own feelings and so they can never emotionally grow or learn. This family is supporting their father in his inability to control his temper, in his refusal to be accountable for his behaviour and his emotional immaturity. They are not helping themselves or him by their desire 'not to make him angry' in any way at all.

When you love and accept people without taking on responsibility for their behaviour, without feeling that you must fix them, then you disengage; it is hatred and resentments, jealousy and anger that keeps us attached to people. The more we release and remove hatred, prejudice, fears and resentments, the more room we have for love and light. You can love people in your own way, being authentic to yourself without having to change them or having them change you. That does not mean there is no compromise, discussion or flexibility within relationships; it is not that we should become totally selfish. It is a realisation that you are responsible for your emotions and feelings and how you behave when experiencing them. It is a feeling of love and respect. That is reverence for yourself and others.

Happiness Leads to Becoming Love™

Since ancient times, our heart is thought to be, at least on an energetic level, where our love comes from. Scientists at the HeartMath Institute in California have shown that more information is sent to the brain from the heart, than from the brain to the heart. So, it makes sense to keep our hearts healthy so we can function and Become Love more easily. Happiness is the key to an emotionally healthy heart and in those moments in your life when you are truly happy there is no room for worry, stress, fears or resentments. Realising happiness in your life is showing yourself reverence.

I want you to think now of moments in your life when you are truly happy, when it feels like time stops still in your moment of sheer bliss, when you can live in the moment of happiness and feel love for the moment in every heartbeat. There is a space for you to write down when you have had these moments or what things you do in your life which give you these feelings, so you can remember to do more of them!

When are you truly happy?

The more we pursue happiness, the more we make time for these moments, and the more we clear belief systems that prevent us from being happy, the easier it is to Become Love. So now having made these notes, revisit them from time to time, and make a conscious decision to find more of these moments of happiness in your life.

Our hearts are powerful. They can help us access our inner wisdom to show us what we can do in our lives to help us achieve happiness. If you could speak to your heart, what would your heart want to tell you? What does it want you to do more of to be happy? The following exercise will allow you to find out.

Exercise: *Speak to the Heart*

This exercise is designed to assist you in acquiring certain feelings that will help you to Become Love by understanding what happiness and joy are, and by allowing yourself to really listen to your heart.

Firstly, take a pen and read the statements of feelings below. Circle YES to any of them that you would like to feel or think you already do feel. The second part of this exercise is to make yourself comfortable and listen to the second meditation on the **Becoming Love™ Meditation Album**, *Speak to the Heart*. All of these feelings below are included on *track 2*, **Speak to the Heart Meditation,** which you can listen to and enjoy now, later and as many times as you like. So, first, read the feeling statements and circle YES if you think you already do feel this or would like to feel this.

Feeling work on Happiness and Joy: Speak to the Heart

Feelings You May Have or May Wish to Have	Circle the word YES if you would like to have this feeling or feel you already do have it.
I already know how to be, and what it feels like to be, happy and full of joy.	YES
I already know how to be, and what it feels like to be, content.	YES
I already know how to be joyful and what it feels like to experience joy.	YES
I already know it is possible to make time in my life to pursue the things that make me happy.	YES
I am allowed to make time in my life to pursue the things that make me happy; I know how to and I am worthy and deserving of doing so.	YES
I already know how to be, and what it feels like to be, happy for others.	YES
I already know how to be, and what it feels like to be, happy for others without…	
…. comparing myself to others.	YES
…. being jealous of others.	YES
…. feeling I am missing out.	YES
…. feeling stupid.	YES
…. feeling unworthy.	YES
…. feeling lesser than them.	YES

Meditation: *Speak to the Heart*

The second part of this exercise is a joyful meditation, ***Speak to the Heart***, which allows you to take time to listen to your own heart. During the meditation you will imagine going into a space in your heart and asking your heart what it really wants right now in your life. Maybe this will be your way of discovering what your 'God dream' is. That dream that asks, if money were really no object, what you would want to have in your life. This is a huge dream that may seem impossible now but I want you to have the feeling that all things are possible; it is just that we may not understand how right now. You may be shown something in your life that will form part of your learning to Becoming Love™.

Whatever it is your heart is telling you, you will hear and listen to it. This may not feel like 'hearing' in your ears, or 'seeing' like a film. It may be like a knowing or a feeling. In whatever way you receive the information, it is valid for you. You will remember whatever is important and there is space to write it down afterwards. During the meditation you will hear my voice guiding you into a deep relaxed state, reminding you of these feelings you circled YES to above, and inviting you to imagine speaking to your heart.

> Make yourself comfortable in a quiet place where you will not be disturbed for about 30 minutes. You could sit or lie down. Now, listen to the ***Speak to the Heart Meditation*** which is *track 2,* on the **Becoming Love™ Meditation Album.**
>
> All of the feelings in the exercise above are included on this 2nd meditation; as you listen to it, you can just allow the sound of my voice to wash over you and relax. You don't need to respond if you hear me asking you a question because by completing the questions above you have already made your intentions clear, but if you choose to affirm or not in your head, you can do so. Relax and enjoy now!

Write your experiences in this space so that you remember what your heart is telling you it desires now, so you can feel more happiness in your life, and so find it easier to Become Love.

Speak to the Heart: My Heart Showed me.........

Being true to yourself, to your own heart and soul, being your authentic self and keeping your vibration high, raises others' vibrations. Never sink to the vibration of the drama, the competition, the ego, but keep yours high; you can only rise to the level of love to the extent you allow your lack of love for others to hold you back. Fear, anger, hate, emotional pain and resentment can all be healed with love.

Releasing Resentments

Now I want to draw your attention to some of the negative feelings that are weighing you down or, in other words, lowering your vibration and so inhibiting your ability to have reverence for others. What *is* your vibration? When I think of a person's vibration, I am referring to the energy they are reflecting inwards to themselves and outwards to others by their thoughts, words, actions and behaviour. I imagine that negative emotions such as hatred, anger, resentment and jealousy are heavy and lower our vibration, whereas positive emotions such as joy, kindness, courage and of course, love are light and raise our vibration.

Perhaps you have heard of the concept of the 'law of attraction'? In this ideology, it is said that the energy you put out to the Universe will be matched by the same energies and sent back to you. Imagine the universe being like a mirror. If you send out negative vibrations, you will receive more negative vibrations, and if you send out positive vibes, you will get positive ones returned. In my experience there is one word which sums this up and ensures you shine out brightly and receive back with joy - alignment. Keeping your vibration high, being in alignment with love ensures you get more love back.

> *'Everything is energy and that's all there is to it. Match the frequency of the reality you want and you cannot help but get that reality. It can be no other way. This is not philosophy. This is physics.'*
>
> Albert Einstein

If you see the truth you will revere; if you revere, you will see the truth. They are intertwined. Accepting the truth will really allow you to see people without judging them. Of course, it is our human nature to notice others' behaviour, words and actions. We often then form an opinion about that person from that observation without understanding their motivations or the full picture, or without understanding the truth of a situation. Naturally, we notice others and how they behave, but forming judgements about them from our observations can lead us to harbour negative thoughts: resentment; prejudice; anger; hatred and fear.

If and when you find you are judging someone, then you are probably learning something from them. For example, if you feel that your neighbour is constantly showing you how wealthy he is by mentioning his next holiday, inviting you to admire his new car, moaning about his builders who are not building his enormous extension to time, mentioning how expensive his wife's tastes are with an indulgent smile, etc., etc., then you may form the judgement that he is boastful, arrogant and just a bit of a 'show off'. So, what is his behaviour teaching you? At the very least, you are learning not to be like him as it not a likeable personality trait.

Once you acknowledge that you can 'learn the lesson', then you can let it go. You will find *he* is the same, but the way you react to him is now different. Instead of finding him irritating, you find his postulating humorous which just might mean you take the time to relax and get to know him better. Maybe then you will find out a little more about him and his situation. And yes, he may still just be a bit of a show off but you can accept him as he is, choosing to spend time with him or not. Or maybe you find out that it is all a big act because he has his own insecurities and as you get to know him better and he feels accepted by you, he becomes more authentic with you. So, whether you learn one thing or many from your own judgements, finding out what you are 'learning' by judging, accepting the lesson consciously, letting the judgement and negativity go, and accepting the other person as they are, will free you from heavy negative feelings and help you keep your vibration high and Become Love.

Exercise: *Releasing resentments and judgements*

This exercise will allow you to think about who you might resent and why; in doing so you will be able to release some negativity towards them and feel lighter, without feeling diminished. In the space below, write down some people or groups of people that you know you have formed negative judgements about. Note what it is they do or say which really annoys you, and what *positive* things you think you are learning by noticing this annoying behaviour. Remember it could be one thing or many things. Write down as many as you like but don't feel bad. It is perfectly normal human behaviour and no one is going to see this except you.

Who are you Judging?	What is it that is Annoying About Them?	What can you Learn from This Behaviour?
EXAMPLE *My friend*	*He borrows money from me and others, and never repays it in full.*	1. *How to say 'No' without feeling guilty.* 2. *How to be assertive and kind.* 3. *How to be discerning about whom to lend money to.* 4. *How to have and express empathy or sympathy for another, without having to give them money.*

> *Now take each person or group of people in turn and look at what you have written. Consciously tell yourself that you 'already know that now, so you don't need to learn it from being aggravated by their behaviour any longer.' Close your eyes, take a deep breath in and out, relax and, as you do so, feel that resentment releasing from your body.*

This simple acknowledging and releasing exercise is useful during our daily lives too, and can be practised in a moment when you feel yourself being overwhelmingly irritated or annoyed. It may not change their behaviour but it changes the way you react to them and feel within yourself; less stress is always good for you!

I am constantly amazed at how some people react to each other, feeling stressed, easily annoyed or riled by other people who are just being who they are. You don't have to allow yourself to feel this highly emotional. Opening yourself up to love is so relaxing, you are not condoning and you don't have to be around those people but accepting without judging is easy and we can all learn how to do it. We can shine this feeling of love out to others, which not only is felt and helps them, but it helps you too, as you feel the acceptance within and of yourself and of others.

Relax your inner self and allow peace to come in.

Shining Love from the Heart

Exercise: *Shining Love to Humanity*

This exercise is designed to assist you in acquiring certain feelings that will help you to Become Love by understanding what reverence for humanity feels like and by learning to shine out that love.

Firstly, take a pen and read the statements of feelings below. Circle YES to any of them that you would like to feel or think you already do feel. The second part of this exercise is to make yourself comfortable and listen to the third meditation on the **Becoming Love™ Meditation Album**. All of these feelings below are included on *track 3*, ***Shining love to Humanity Meditation***, which you can listen to and enjoy now, later and as many times as you like.

Feeling work on Shining Love to Humanity

Feelings You Already Have or Would Like to Have	Circle the word YES if you would like to have this feeling or feel you already do have it.
I understand what humanity is from the highest perspective, and my perception and understanding are the same.	YES
I already understand what a human is and that I am a human being.	YES
I already know I am, and what it feels like to be, part of humanity.	YES
To Love...	
I already know what it feels like to love and revere all of humanity.	YES
I already know it is possible to love and revere all of humanity.	YES
I already know it is possible to love and revere all of humanity without feeling drained or running out of energy.	YES
I already know I am able to love and revere all of humanity.	YES
I already feel worthy and deserving of loving and revering all of humanity.	YES
To be loved and revered by...	
I already know what it feels like to be loved and revered by other people.	YES

I already know it is possible to be loved and revered by other people.	YES
I already know it is possible to be loved and revered by other people without…	
… without being drained.	YES
… without being overwhelmed.	YES
… without being judged.	YES
… without being tricked.	YES
… without being betrayed.	YES
… without being marginalised.	YES
… without being stepped on or stepped over.	YES
… without being walked over.	YES
… without being invisible.	YES
I already know how to be loved and revered by other people.	YES
I already know I am worthy and deserving of being loved and revered by other people.	YES

Meditation: *Shining Love to Humanity*

> Make yourself comfortable in a quiet place where you will not be disturbed for about 30 minutes. You could sit or lie down. Now, listen to the ***Shining Love to Humanity Meditation*** which is *track 3,* on the **Becoming Love™ Meditation Album.**
>
> All of the feelings in the exercise above are included on this meditation; as you listen to it, you can just allow the sound of my voice to wash over you and relax. You don't need to respond if you hear me asking you a question because by completing the questions above you have already made your intentions clear, but if you choose to affirm or not in your head, you can do so. Relax and enjoy now!

Remember that you can shine love to humanity in your day to day life, every day, whenever you choose to. I remind myself of this every day by using this active affirmation exercise. It reinforces the meditation that you have just listened to. You can try this now and include it in your daily routine. I use it first thing in the morning before I get out of bed as it makes a great start to my day and puts me in a loving frame of mind to work with other people.

Exercise: *Shining Love to Humanity Affirmation*

Read or recite these words and follow the breathing instructions:

> *'I am love. I radiate love. I shine love. Everyone I come across today will see this and feel this; they will know I love them, that I value them. They will feel that I see their souls and their hearts and that I revere them. I will see the virtues they have, their goodness, their innocence, I will see the truth and I love them.'*
>
> *Now, breathe in love and hold that thought. Breathe out love and feel it radiating out of you. Breathe in love and breathe out love and feel it showing in your eyes. Breathe in love. Breathe out love and feel it showing in your smile. Breathe in love. Breathe out love and hear it in your voice, the words that you speak and the tone that you speak in. Breathe in love. Breathe out love and feel yourself radiating love.'*

Allowing Love to Come Through You

Allowing love to come through you, by feeling it coming into you from the universe around you, accepting that feeling and allowing it to shine out to others, is the easiest way to Become Love. We are sparks of love. We are tiny sparks of the huge energy of unconditional love that is all around us. As a network of humanity, we are capable of love; we are love. There is no need to try so hard to harness love or to hold onto it with jealously or with fear. Just allow love to come through you, to be the energy of you, allow yourself to be love.

We are a part of creation, a part of nature; we are natural beings and are divinely entitled to accept this gift of love peacefully. Becoming Love™ can be effortless. You can leave positivity everywhere you go and touch everyone you meet. Just as Galileo described the sun in the beautiful quotation below, you can shine out to others with no extra effort in your life.

> *'The sun with all those planets revolving around it and dependent on it, can still ripen a bunch of grapes as if it had nothing else in the universe to do.'*
>
> Galileo

Shining out love to others is a joyful way of Becoming Love™ and feeling a deep reverence for humanity. You will see people for who they are. So not as the grumpy bus driver or the impatient shop keeper, not as customers who are buying your services, but as souls who you love, who are on a journey just like you are.

Allowing love to flow through you means you can set boundaries with love without having to shield yourself with fear or anger. Love radiating out of you is the best boundary against emotional hurt. In an uncomfortable situation the ego, left unchecked, perhaps feeling bruised from years of fear, anxiety and lack of self-love, reacts in counterproductive way.

Imagine being snapped at by a work colleague or a friend for no apparent reason other than they are having a bad day and you were in the wrong place at the wrong time. Your thought process might go something like this….

What did s/he do that for?

I will give her/him a piece of my mind!

How _dare_ they?

I will _never_ forgive her/him.

But..., well......, I must be a worthless person/ unworthy of respect/ disliked/ in the wrong, for them to treat me like that....... It must be my fault.

I should have shouted back/defended myself, but I didn't because I am too weak and pathetic.

I am pathetic and useless. No wonder people shout at me.

In this example, by the end of this short event, not only have you been shouted at for no apparent reason but now you think it is your fault and you deserve that kind of treatment.

In half a minute, from one simple interaction with another fellow human, our own ego can have us spinning in circles. Allowing yourself to come from love is a boundary to prevent these kinds of interactions and the follow up self-demeaning thought patterns. What about if we re-run that scenario....

You get shouted at for no apparent reason by a friend or a work colleague and you recognise immediately the truth of the situation. You are not in the wrong, it is just that they are having a really bad time and feeling stressed. Of course, they shouldn't snap at you but they did, and now you can address it with assertiveness, kindness and love. You can disarm and diffuse the situation with love without being weak or vulnerable.

How about if you had responded in one of these ways?

Are you okay? How can I help?

Hold on a minute, I can see you are really angry. Is there anything I can do?

Are you alright? I tell you what, I'll come back later.

Smile, look them in the eyes, know it is 'their stuff' not yours, and offer to help or retreat with politeness, assertiveness and kindness.

When you are coming from love, with reverence for everyone, you react with love and you can diffuse negativity for yourself and often for the others in the situation too. You are a miracle worker, changing the planet one person at a time. If you show reverence to one person or one living being today you can change their life. It is as simple as that. This old tale is one of my favourite stories:

> *'Once upon a time there was a man and a woman walking along the shoreline. The sand was littered in starfish which had been beached and were drying out in the hot sun, unable to get back to the sea, because the tide was going out. Every so often the woman bent down, picked up a starfish and gently tossed it back into the ocean. After watching her for some time, the man asked her why she was bothering. There were hundreds of starfish, she couldn't possibly save them all. 'That's true,' she replied, 'but it makes a difference to this one, (she throws it in) and this one, (she throws another in,) and this one......'*
>
> *Anon*

You can make a difference to one person's life today; and that person can be you or anyone else you meet. So, allow yourself to act with reverence, for yourself and others, and make a difference to someone, somewhere today.

Heart to Heart Hugging

Our hearts are our life force on a physical level, and ancient cultures believed that this miraculous muscular organ was the most important in our bodies, not just from a physical stance but also emotionally and spiritually. For example, the ancient Egyptians when mummifying their dead took great care to preserve the heart (as well as some other body parts) in its own special embalming jar, whereas the mushy grey matter in the skull was thrown out. The brain was not deemed important enough to be preserved for the dead person on their journey into the underworld. Wherever you stand regarding the importance of the heart organ to us emotionally and spiritually, it would appear that humans instinctively feel something primal about this organ and react to its rhythm.

For example, when a baby is upset and its mother holds it, she will often subconsciously match their heart beats so that the baby feels safe. When a mother is afraid or stressed, the baby picks up on the fast heartbeat and becomes distressed. If you pick up a crying baby and remain calm, and consciously slow your breathing, the baby will soon relax. When our hearts are in rhythm with other's hearts, we feel less stressed. Some people find the beating of Native American or African drums triggers fear, perhaps deep in their cellular memory from long ago times. If this happens and you consciously change your body's rhythm to that of the drums, you will find that you no longer feel so afraid.

What would happen if your heart beat matched the heartbeat of everyone else you met today in that moment? One of the greatest ways to spread love and feel loved is by heart to heart hugging. This is something you can do with people you already know and love, in order to get the feeling of this wonderful connection.

Are you one of those who waits fearfully as you are approached by an old friend who is rushing forward with open arms to sweep you into a huge hug? Do you awkwardly pat the back of someone who hugs you, counting the seconds until they release you? In my seminars, students walk around the room and practise this with each other on the first day. Of course, it feels weird! It is not accepted behaviour, especially in many of our cultures, to hug strangers but after the initial embarrassment, the feeling of agape wins over and students feel the connection between each other.

It took me a long time to enjoy being hugged or to hug others. As a child I felt violated if anyone including my family tried to hug me and would stand, rigid, waiting for it to stop. It felt as if they wanted something from me that I was unable to give. As I grew older I chose to hug or be hugged by some and that felt good but I was still very awkward about being hugged by most people. I don't remember who hugged me and helped me recognise a different type of affection shown through a hug but I do know it felt that I was loved and accepted freely without having to give anything back or do anything. I learnt it was possible to feel complete unconditional love (agape) through a hug. Over time I have changed and I think many people who have only known me in the last 10 years would describe me as a hugger; I want others to feel that reverence through touch. It has taken me a lifetime so far to give and receive in this way, so be patient with yourself. The more you love and accept yourself, the more you can share the love.

For the next exercise, I am not advising you to rush out and find a stranger. Please don't! Choose someone you already know and love, with their permission of course!

Exercise: *Heart to Heart Hugging*

Find someone you like and hug them, heart to heart. When you hug, you move to the right so your heart is in front of their heart. Hold the hug and feel their heart beating. Consciously match your heart beat by changing your breathing. Feel the unity with that person and notice how connected and warm it feels to be embraced. If you do this with an intimate partner you can really allow yourself to sink into the feeling and reach a wonderful sense of connection.

How did you find the heart to heart hugging? How do you find hugging in general? How do you feel right now about feeling reverence for everyone you meet?

Becoming Love™

Write down your feelings and experiences…

Exercise: *Beliefs Around Reverence*

You may have belief systems or programmes that could be holding you back from Becoming Love™.

Stand up and test the beliefs below, as you learnt in Chapter 1. Remember to ensure that you are testing YES/NO correctly, to speak aloud and have your eyes closed.

	Belief to Check	Desired Response	Your check mark*
	To Love...		
1	I love humanity	Yes	
2	I am afraid or scared to love humanity,	No	
3	The more I love, the more visible I become.	No*	
4	The more I love, the more invisible I become.	No*	
	To be Loved...		
5	I am afraid or scared to be loved by humanity.	No	
	To Revere...		
6	I revere humanity.	Yes	
7	I am afraid or scared to revere humanity.	No	
	To be Revered...		
8	I am revered by humanity.	Yes	
9	I am afraid or scared to be revered by humanity.	Yes	

(*You are looking for a 'No' here because your visibility should not be linked to your ability to love!)

If you do hold any of these potentially limiting beliefs or programmes, and you will probably hold many of them, don't panic! By the time you have read this book, practised the exercises and listened to the meditations, you will already be much closer to Becoming Love™ and you will have already changed these beliefs within you. You can come back to them at the end and retest the ones you thought you held and enjoy witnessing the transformation. (You do not need to test those you never held in the first place, just the ones you originally marked.) If after this you find you are still holding some of these beliefs or if you would like to clear them faster, there are different ways of doing this which I have talked about in chapter 1. This is 'big stuff' and if you can feel yourself getting irritated, overwhelmed, angry or sad, allow yourself to learn and grow, knowing you are safe and loved. The more we deal with our own emotions, which you are doing by working with and through Becoming Love™, the less we experience these feelings, and the more we can experience reverence for others. In the words of Rumi, who expresses this so well:

> *'Your task is not to seek for love, but merely to seek and find all the barriers within yourself that you have built against it.'*
> Rumi

How to Keep Your 'Vibration' High

Keeping your vibration high is a sure-fire way to increase your self-love and ensure your own happiness, and so to feel love for others. In the 1990's, Vianna Stibal created The New Life Experiment ideology. It is a set of ideas that people can aim to live by to assist in being and feeling full of 'lite' thoughts. Imagine our bodies as vessels. If we consciously fill our minds and hearts with positive emotions then we will have less room for negativity. The New Life Experiment is not a set of rules and it is not expected that any one of us can follow its guidance exactly all the time. It is a set of ideas which we can choose to work towards. It isn't easy immediately, but it gets easier.

Whenever you find or hear yourself gossiping or whining, or criticising or moaning, or any of the actions on the list, stop yourself. Do it without self-punishment or disappointment but just with a positive learning attitude. Take a look at the New Life Experiment and see what you think. It may seem a huge ask – but no one is asking you to try it, it is up to you! There are no prizes and no punishment. It is just for you to read and take note of. If you would then like to take the message on board and have a go, do so. It is an ongoing way of being. You will, over time find it is easier and you will find you feel lighter, more positive, more loved and more loving towards others. It will assist you in Becoming Love™.

This lifestyle choice is designed to train ourselves to self-monitor what we say, what we do, how we act and react to others. This ideology will show you just how much negativity that we create in our lives and how we can stop ourselves from saying and doing negative things.

The New Life Experiment

Things to Remember:
No complaining.
No whining.
No being overly critical.
No being overly judgemental.
No poking fun at others.
No being cynical or facetious.
No creating reasons to be sorry or to say you're sorry out of habit.
No creating reasons to stress.
No creating reasons to be unhappy.
No affirming negative thoughts, such as 'I'm overweight.'
No affirming negative feelings, such as 'I'm depressed.'
No making reasons to be angry.
No making or seeking out reasons to overcome, to fight, to struggle, or combat (more than necessary).
No making reasons to be anxious.
No making reasons to be overwhelmed.
No making reasons to worry.
No making reasons for self-doubt.
No creating situations of lack or scarcity with statements such as 'I don't have enough energy,' instead make the claim 'I have plenty'.
No creating chaos or drama for entertainment, excitement, adventure, thrills, or to avoid peace.
No wrong or right, better or worse, should, hope or try.

Vianna Stibal

When you catch yourself using a negative statement, always change it. Better yet, catch yourself before you say it and choose a different thought. Shift to a different reality and choose to use your energy on more positive things. Negative thought forms consume an incredible amount of our energy. As the negative thought form begins to take shape, stop it in motion and back up, change your thought to a more positive one instantly.

This is an ongoing way of life and a learning process; be kind to yourself and allow yourself to learn these new habits. This is what I mean when I speak of keeping your vibration high; be positive, change your negative thought patterns to positive ones and show love for yourself and others. Allowing love to flow through you every day keeps your vibration high, and others will rise to match yours. Never be afraid to look into your own heart, be your own best friend, who loves without judging and allow yourself to see, to learn and to move forward clearly.

Experiencing Love for Humanity

The next exercise is a meditation that allows you to feel and experience the feeling of love for humanity with loving boundaries. It has similarities to a Buddhist loving-kindness (Metta Bhavana) meditation which can be used to practise feeling compassion for others. This is a beautiful, gentle, meditative exercise that you can do every morning; it will balance your energy and allow you to go into your day with a loving attitude towards yourself and others.

Meditation: *Feeling Your Way to Love*

> Make yourself comfortable in a quiet place where you will not be disturbed for about 20 minutes. You could sit or lie down. Now, listen to the **Experiencing Love for Humanity Meditation** which is *track 4*, on the **Becoming Love™ Meditation Album.**
>
> As you listen, you can just allow the sound of my voice to wash over you and relax. You don't need to respond if you hear me asking you a question but if you choose to, you can do so. Relax and enjoy now!

A script for this meditation is written below so you can read it too if you prefer.

> *Make yourself comfortable in your chair or lying down. Centre yourself in your heart, close your eyes and imagine energy coming up from the centre of the earth through the soles of your feet. Imagine it travelling up your body, up your spine, balancing and aligning you, all the way to the top of your head. Imagine sending your consciousness out of the top of our head, out into the universe, through layers of light. Keep going up through all the layers of light and through a great, big layer of bright golden light. Go through this, through a jelly like substance that has all the colours of the rainbow in it and up into a tingly, white, effervescent light. This light is unconditional love. Imagine going deep within it and feel it coming through your body. You can feel that you are at one with this energy. Feel and know that you are this unconditional love. Now imagine the energy within your own body and know that you are part of it and it is part of you. Imagine you are this unconditional love; part of this deep reverence, this agape.*

> *All this energy is within you. It is you. Feel it now and feel connected to it on every level and in every molecule in your body. Then imagine you expand out so your loving energy has become at one with everyone else in the building. Imagine that your molecules are transferring back and forth between each other. You are not stretching, you have just expanded. Now imagine that you expand further into your community. Imagine your loving energy becoming as one with all the people in your local community. Notice how you feel love for them as you become one. Now expand out to all the people in your state or your country. Allow yourself to feel love for everyone. You are spreading love as you expand. Now imagine your love spreading out all over the world, to every single person on the planet. Feel the humanity. Know that you are part of humanity. Feel it. Feel the connection, the love, the acceptance and the reverence. Feel your love for them and their love for you because you are part of one network of humanity. You are all sparks of unconditional loving energy. You are all unconditional love. Now take a deep breath in. Breathe in love. Breathe out love. Know you are love and that you are loved. Open your eyes.*

The technique used to allow you to easily access a relaxed meditative state is the ThetaHealing® road map developed by Vianna Stibal.

Your connection to the highest energy in our universe, in my words, to Creator, is key to the treasure of Becoming Love™, to learning to love yourself and so to loving humanity, but it is not the whole story. Faith is important to your ability to feel this connection, and faith is an aspect of love. The stronger you feel connected to the unconditional loving energy that is all around us, the more easily you will see and feel the higher truth, you will recognise your own truth and see others' truth. This picture of 'truths' or perspectives, allows you to have reverence for the other person and their position in any situation.

The stronger our feeling of connection, the more we have access to the energy of everything; to deep wisdom, to creativity and to limitless possibilities, so we can do and be anything. But you have to know *what* to do, and *who* to be, and this is where love comes in. Love is a many faceted jewel of a virtue, and within each facet there is a further set of facets. I see love as an intertwined, interrelated set of virtues. Mastering these aspects of love, behaving in a way that celebrates them, speaking with them, listening with them, touching with them, allows us to use the treasure that is the energy of everything all around us, which is just pure love.

CHAPTER 4

How to Be Yourself and Love Yourself

If you allow yourself to be yourself, who you truly are, without fear of judgement, you will find it easier to love yourself and you will feel as if the universe is supporting you more. You can't be anyone else, so be you! It doesn't matter what anyone else is doing or how they are doing it. Do it your way! What are you good at? What are you an expert in? What feels comfortable for you? Allow yourself to be true to be you. It's so much easier!

The more you are your authentic self, the more you will love yourself, because you are being authentic and honest with yourself. The more you love yourself, the more you will be able to love others easily. Perhaps this is another example of how in the English language we are lacking in enough words to describe love. There is a huge difference between the ego driven energy of loving yourself, becoming selfish, narcissistic and driven only by your own needs, and the energy of loving yourself from the perspective of the energy of unconditional love.

How can you learn to love yourself from this perspective? How do you love yourself without becoming selfish or arrogant? How do you let go and love yourself without fearing you will become selfish or arrogant, or that people will think you are selfish or arrogant? How do you know where to start? I have 7 top tips to assist you in learning and maintaining an unconditional, honest, humble yet proud, inspiring, motivating and forgiving love for yourself. A love which will be your starting point to Becoming Love™. The more you love yourself in this true sense, the more you will be able to love others completely.

7 Top Tips to Being your Authentic Self and Loving Yourself.

1. Be self-full!

2. Notice what you are doing for others.

3. Consider your regrets and how you can address them.

4. Practise self-compassion and self-nurture.

5. Be true to your life purpose.

6. Have balance in your life.

7. Self-Acceptance.

Number One in my top tips to being your Authentic Self and Loving Yourself: **Be Self-full**

We use the expression *selfish* and the expression *selfless* without having a word to explain the middle ground. In the English language we have almost more words than any other language in the world. (Sadly, however, most native speakers rarely use more than a tenth of them on a regular basis – but that is a whole other discussion!) In our expansive vocabulary we have a word to describe people who think only of themselves; that word is *selfish*. We also have a word to describe those who think of others before themselves all the time, and that word is *selfless*. There is nothing in between! No dictionary defined word to describe the vast gulf between selfishness and selflessness. Initially one might suppose that one is wrong and the other is right, so there is no need for a middle ground. Selfishness is bad, isn't it? So, selflessness must be good, mustn't it? Actually, I don't think so. I believe that both ways of being are as limiting as each other in different ways.

Someone who is entirely selfish may initially have life the way they want it because they always put their needs first. However, because they put their needs first all the time, their way of life is usually detrimental to others in some aspect. So invariably they end up without a circle of support from friends or family who have become fed up with them over time, and they often end up lonely and unhappy. On the other hand, those who are entirely selfless may initially be praised by others for their kindness, service and unfailing support. They may feel good about devoting their life to others. However, over time, those being supported by this selfless person become less appreciative as they come to expect the constant help and rely on the supporter to continue to provide it. This pattern of behaviour snowballs until, with no time spent on their own needs, the selfless person becomes exhausted and resentful as their needs are never met (by themselves or anyone else). They may become bitter and unhappy as they do not feel appreciated for all the things they do for others.

So, I use a new expression to describe a more comfortable way of being which is the middle ground between selfish and selfless. I call it being *self-full*! The best way to illustrate self-fullness is this: imagine being on an aeroplane, sitting next to a toddler when the plane starts to move around violently, and the oxygen masks come down from the overhead panel. If you attempted to put the mask on the frightened child first, you may well end up in a deadly struggle as they thrash about in fear. This could end in tragedy for both of you. If, however you put your own oxygen mask on first as recommended, which will take you a matter of seconds, then you are in a safe position to calmly help the frightened child. Of course, I can hear some of you saying that the child may just keep pulling his mask off anyway out of fear, however calm and reassuring you are. That is true; but you are in a much better position to reason or control them and if the worst comes to the worst, without wishing to be harsh, at least one of you has survived and you know you did your utmost to help them live.

In applying this analogy to your day to day life, you only need to ensure that you have a balance. You should consider meeting your own needs so that you are better placed to support others if you choose to. Do you know when you need to rest and when you can work efficiently? Do you have appropriate boundaries and are you able to say 'No' with love and without guilt? Do you know that your needs, your time and your desires, are equally as important as others'? Not *more* important but *as* important. Recognising and applying this is especially difficult for some of us and incredibly easy for others – and this in itself causes resentment amongst those of us who have been consistently selfless in the past. Often selfless people are incredibly resentful of selfish people and that prevents them from being able to access self-fullness.

Some of us who are essentially selfless, look around and see others balancing themselves in the middle, being self-full and mistakenly think they are also selfish. Is it because *you* would like to be in this comfortable middle ground, but you feel guilty if you don't do everything for everyone else? I believe that consistently doing everything for everyone can be disempowering for the receiver. By being entirely selfless and picking up the pieces for your family and friends, jumping in to rescue them, covering for them, devoting your time to supporting them whenever they ask, you can actually be doing them a big disservice. They never learn to support themselves, to problem solve, to grow emotionally, to be independent or to be self-reliant, self-motivating or take responsibility for themselves.

It is also apparent, and not very comfortable to recognise, that on some level, we are being selfless for a selfish motivation. Do you feel that you are only included or loved if you do things for others devotedly? Working through this book will assist you in recognising that you are worthy and deserving of being loved for who you are and want to be, not because you drop everything to babysit when you are asked to or agree with everything your colleagues say so they feel intelligent. Wouldn't you like to know you are loved and feel loved because you are awesome just as you are? Would you like to feel that people will love and include you, even when you allow yourself to meet your own needs, speak your truth and be authentic?

Loving yourself empowers you to be self-full. The more you practise being self-full, the more interesting your life becomes and the more interesting you become, and others will love you because *you* love you. I had an interesting interaction with an acquaintance recently where this was very apparent. She was upset that she missed her weekly coffee morning at her book club because she had had so much of her son's ironing to do and he needed to collect it the next day. I asked her when she was going to stop doing her 30-year olds son's ironing. Her son lives alone, has a great job managing a team of people and an active social life. She explained that he doesn't know how to iron and likes his work shirts to look 'really smart'. Obviously, he can't iron as well as her – she has 45 years of experience and he has never had to learn! She acknowledged that she sees it as a chance to see him, but as he would usually let himself in to her house, dump the washing and then come back later to collect it when she would be on her evening work shift, in reality, the whole social interaction was never very worthwhile or very long. Instead of grumbling over his washing pile, I suggested she show him how to do it for himself or recommend a great local laundry and then stop doing it for him. She had to assert herself with kindness and recognise that she could empower him to take charge of his own laundry, love herself enough to go to her favourite weekly event and arrange a mutually convenient time to see her son when they both had time to sit down and chat. At first, she protested because he was *so* busy, he probably wouldn't be able to find a 'convenient time.' However, as we chatted, she concluded that by doing his ironing she was treating him as a teenager; it was a pattern that had begun when he was a student but now she was a parent of an adult. She needed to treat him like one and communicate her needs to him, adult to adult, and arrange quality time with him. How did it go? Well he was a little miffed at first. The arrangement had suited them both so he thought but, once he realised that she was sacrificing her time to support him in this way, he was apologetic; it had never occurred to him to change the arrangement for her benefit. He was more than happy to learn how to do his laundry and now they have a regular supper which is far more enjoyable for both of them

Your first step to loving yourself more is not seeking to become selfish, but to become self-full. By attending to your own needs, you are better placed to support others if you choose to. When you give yourself what you want, whether it be a walk on a sunny day, time to curl up on the sofa and read a book, or buy yourself a bunch of flowers, whatever it is, you instantly feel happier. You feel gratitude for your life and the universe, acting like the mirror that it is, gives back. It reflects back what you have already and gives you more. So being a little self-full allows you to become more self-full. If you need to rest, rest. If you are energised or inspired to do something, do it. Follow your natural rhythm as far as you can and practise self-fullness. Being self-full means attending to your needs and wishes so you are in a strong position to attend to others' needs and wishes.

> Being self-full is a way of loving yourself so you can love others more. It is a 'win win' way of living your life!

Selfless   **SELF-FULL**   Selfish

Would you like to understand the meaning and perspective of self-fullness and to be able to apply it in your day to day life? To really understand what that feels like? Would you like to know that being self-full is a way of living your life in balance, so you are happy, well rested and your needs are met, and you are in position to help others if you choose to?

Exercise: *Self-full Planning*

In what ways could you be more self-full? Write down some thoughts and action plans here.

Number two in top tips to Being your Authentic Self and Loving Yourself: **What are you doing for everybody else?**

The support and help you offer others can often be an indication of where you need help and support. For example, if you find yourself volunteering as a hospital visitor, maybe deep down you are lonely or have fears of being alone, or you fear lacking friendship or companionship. It is always a good idea to recognise what you fear so you can address it in whichever way suits you.

Many of us are very good at pretending that everything is okay. The most common phrase you hear in the UK when you ask someone how they are, or how their weekend went is 'Oh, Fine.' It is a suitably bland response that is accepted by the enquirer as a comfortable, positive response and the respondent can safely use this term without fearing they will offend or embarrass the enquirer. If one did in fact have an amazing weekend, it is socially acceptable to say so as long as your enthusiasm does not tip over into bragging or boasting. If, however, your life is not great for you, it is not considered socially acceptable to say so, for fear of putting the enquirer in an awkward position. Hearing your negative response, they would have to 'do something' about your problem or distress. At the very least they would have to show sympathy and it would be uncomfortable for both parties. So, all over the UK every day, you hear phrases such as: 'I'm fine'; 'Its fine'; 'Oh, fine;'. These phrases are banded about all over the country thousands of times a day.

To maintain social niceties, one could argue, it's fine (!) to use this code, but if you are constantly putting out the message that you are okay when you are not, are you actually aware of your life and your own happiness at all? Are you being truly honest with yourself? If you are not happy, if you never have a 'really great' weekend, or if you want to live a more content life than you currently do, then it is important that you recognise where your needs are not being met and meet them as far as you can. A first step to doing this is to recognise what you do for others and ask yourself why you do that and is this an area in your life that you could address so you are more content? That doesn't mean you stop helping others in the way that you are currently doing so, but it does mean you start helping yourself too in the same sort of way. The following exercise will assist you in addressing this issue.

Exercise: *Serving Your Own Needs as You Serve Others' Needs*

What do you do for others? How do you serve others' needs?	Does this highlight a need or fear in you?	How could you address or serve your own needs or fears?
Example 1: *I drop everything and give time to my friends when they need me.*	*I want to be supported by my friends when I need it.*	*I can allow myself to call on my friends for support without feeling guilty or needy.*
Example 2: *I volunteer to help at all the events at my child's school.*	*I want to feel included and important in my child's life.*	*I can forge a stronger communicative relationship with my child directly.*

Number Three in my top tips to being your Authentic Self and Loving Yourself: **What Regrets are you holding onto or in Danger of Acquiring?**

This is a very simple philosophy - think about what you might regret if you don't do it.

> *'Thinking about what you might regret can lead to positive decision making about how to lead your life.'*
> Bronnie Ware, Five Biggest Regrets of the Dying

This idea advocates that it is best to lead a life true to yourself, and not to what other people may think of you, or your decisions. For me, this means I aim to be true to my authentic self, and what I feel is my life purpose. By Becoming Love™ you are being true to yourself by practising self-love and supporting yourself.

It is easy to stand still and feel everything is happening around you. Some people never try anything for fear of failure. However, consider this: if you are *not* doing what you really want to now because you fear failing, what is the difference between *not* achieving it now by doing *nothing*, and *doing it* and failing? Nothing! The only difference is that, by not even attempting to do it now, you will always regret it. If you do it and it doesn't work out, then you will find a new way to go but you won't be stuck in your uncomfortable comfort zone thinking about the 'what ifs.'

A colleague one told me that whatever you are doing now, essentially, you are in your comfort zone because otherwise you would be doing something different. Due to my situation at that time, his words were hard to hear but I understood that what he was saying is true. You can have dreams and plans, but unless you actually act on them, you will not achieve them and therefore you are in the stage of planning forever. This planning stage of having ideas, wishing and goal setting is your comfort zone. If you were at ease with actually putting those plans into action, then you would be doing that. We all live in what is our current comfort zone. Do you think that you are more comfortable with planning than actually doing? I suggest that in order to motivate yourself to move forward, you consider what you may regret if you *don't* do it and step out of your comfort zone and …do it!

There is some space below for you to write down some thoughts on what you think you may regret if you don't do. These can be large or small. Do you want to visit the Egyptian pyramids? Do you want to write a book? Do you want to try kayaking? Do you want to learn how to play the guitar? Do you want to sell up and move to the country?

Exercise: *What will you regret if you don't do it?*

What do you Think you will Regret if you don't do it? Write it here.

What about the regrets you already have? Regrets, although essentially negative, can be kept for positive reasons. Very often we subconsciously hold onto regrets to remind us not to take that course of action again or to remember to take a different course of action in the future. This next meditation exercise will help you identify if you are holding onto any of these 'positive regrets', recognise how you can learn from them, and then to release them with love and ease. This is a simple meditation to assist you in highlighting regrets in your life that you are ready to clear, and to show you how you can bring more pleasure into your life as a way of loving yourself.

When I first created this exercise and tried it out for myself, I was surprised by the seemingly insignificant life event that came to mind but how considerably it was impacting me now. During the meditation, I saw myself as a small girl at the piano and then as myself now 'dancing' around in the kitchen whilst I am doing the clearing up. I realised that on some level, I deeply regret giving up learning how to play the piano. I was a thoughtful, creative, intuitive little girl but as I got older I found myself distracted by peers and the pressure I put on myself to do well at school and take 'sensible' subjects and get a 'sensible' job. I then realised that now I get great pleasure from having music playing in the house, but I rarely do play any as I never seem to be bothered to set up my music system and equipment, or download music lists properly! I didn't love myself enough to take the time or be bothered. I recognised within this meditative experience that if one of my family had needed help to sort out their music, I would have dropped what I was doing to assist them; but I had never done it for myself. I simply didn't love myself enough. It took one afternoon to get to grips with iTunes and set up mini speakers and now I have wonderful music playing loudly, often! This exercise in self-nurture which took no time at all has made a big difference to my moments of joy; it has allowed me to love myself more. The meditation allowed me to release the regret of giving up the piano lessons and to make a positive change to my life now. It also showed me how the walls of my tight little comfort zone of doing the 'sensible' thing, which was a safety and security issue in terms of finances, fitting in socially and feeling respected, have definitely expanded, and although I would not consider myself a huge risk taker, I am now living life the way I choose, doing the job I love and leading a fun, exciting lifestyle, whilst knowing and feeling that I am secure and feel safe, respected and accepted.

Meditation: *Release Regrets*

It is time to relax and listen to the *track 5*, the fifth meditation on the **Becoming Love™ Meditation Album**, *Release Regrets*. My words will guide you into a deep meditative state and it is from this deep theta brainwave that we easily connect with our deepest wisdom via the highest energy in our beautiful universe. You may already be aware of some regrets you have and, if so, this exercise may enlighten you as to why you are still holding onto them, or you may find that by doing this meditation, you are surprised what springs into your mind. There is space to write down your thoughts and experiences below either before you listen to the meditation or afterwards, or both!

As with all the meditations included on the **Becoming Love™ Meditation Album**, never try to force an image, just relax and allow whatever comes in to your mind to come in. Never fear you are 'making it up', just accept that your inner intuitive wisdom is showing you what you need to be aware of now. Accept and go with the thoughts, feelings or images you experience. This particular meditation can be emotive, and you may feel like crying as the regret is bought to your attention and released, but just allow yourself to let go. Tears are cleansing in themselves and you are loved.

> Make yourself comfortable in a quiet place where you will not be disturbed for about 30 minutes. You could sit or lie down. Now, listen to the **Release Regrets Meditation** which is *track 5,* on the **Becoming Love™ Meditation Album.**
>
> As you listen to, you can just allow the sound of my voice to wash over you and relax. You don't need to respond if you hear me asking you a question but if you choose to, you can do so. Relax and enjoy now!

Exercise: *My Release Regrets meditation experience*

Write down your experiences from the meditation, here.

Regrets that I am having/ have had	Why I am/was holding onto it and what action I am going to take now

Number Five in my top tips to being your Authentic Self and Loving Yourself: **Self-compassion and Self-nurture**

The more compassion we have for ourselves, the more compassion we can find for others. We are all special. There is no one like you on the planet. So be the best you can be, in your own way. Look after yourself as you would your own best friend, or your own child. Nurture your body, your mind and your soul. We are all unique, but we are all the same – humans with hopes and dreams. If we follow our path with reverence for others, we can connect and create wonderful things together. We can create love. We can hold hands across the world as our authentic selves loving our network of humanity.

Exercise: *Acknowledging my hopes and dreams*

You may want to be alone to do this exercise as it gets quite loud!

> 1. *Firstly think about what you want in life? What do you want to be? What do you want to create for yourself?*
> 2. *Allow yourself to really acknowledge it and take a moment to recognise it....*
> 3. *Now say it in your head!*
> 4. *Now close your eyes and whisper it!*
> 5. *Do it again!*
> 6. *Now say it!*
> 7. *Again!*
> 8. *Now shout it out loud! Again! As many times as you like!*

Would you like to know that you are worthy and deserving of creating whatever you want? Would you like to know how to love yourself enough to do it?

Now write these hopes and dreams down so you can see them.

What I really want for myself is……

Now that it is written, and you have acknowledged you own deepest wishes and desires, allow yourself to feel compassion for yourself. Never quash your own dreams or put yourself down. Encourage and motivate yourself. Of course, you may change your mind and choose another path, hope or dream. However, whether these remain your goals or you move towards others, acknowledging them with self-compassion is the first step to making them real, because you want to for *you*, and you know you deserve it. Some of your goals may be easy for you to start on whereas others may require more planning, but you have already started by acknowledging them with compassion for yourself.

Self-nurture is a learnt virtue; I do consider it a virtue. We learn this type of behaviour from our culture, upbringing, our experiences and the people in our lives. The danger for some of us is that we learnt it in a negative way. How many of you were told as teenagers to stop fussing about with your hair/ stop fiddling with that guitar/get out of the shower/ stop reading that book and come and do this …. some seemingly more virtuous activity? Many of us learnt that paying attention to our need to rest, relax, feel more confident or healthier is selfish or a sign of vanity or laziness.

The advent of social media has accentuated this belief about self-nurture. On the one hand there is a camp of people aghast at how 'celebrities' post their every self-nurturing, self-gratifying minute on social media. Whilst on the other hand, the other camp of people has embraced this wondrous culture and find themselves emulating their heroes as far as they can. Whichever camp you fall into, there is a balance to be attained, but not withstanding extraordinary lifestyles lived out in full view on social media, I am all for self-nurture.

Despite the new fashion of lives being played on social media where self-nurture is encouraged, on the whole most of the people I come across in my mentoring work struggle to find that balance at all and rarely attend to their own needs. Some of the clients I work with have a huge positive social media presence and yet they are deeply unhappy and self-critical on a personal level. Other clients whose lives are more private also find it very, very difficult to nurture themselves. This can be due to lots of reasons from upbringing, culture, personality and experiences. A lady I know in her sweet seventies said she was always exhausted and finding life tiring now. When I asked her about her daily schedule which was full of volunteering roles, housework, dog walking and running errands, it appeared that she rarely stopped to eat until supper time and then afterwards would jump up to clear up, never actually sitting and relaxing at all until after 9pm. When I asked her if she would consider sitting and reading some afternoons, she was shocked – in her world, you just do not do that. 'What would people think if I sat down before 9pm?' I was puzzled as to whom she was referring but I realised that in her social conscience, it is just not acceptable and the 'people' she was referring to were herself and some others, either real or imagined, like her.

Are *you* allowing yourself to nurture yourself the way you would really like to, or are you concerned about what others may think? I'll let you into a secret. Nobody is really that interested in the intricate details of your daily life and if they are aghast that you choose to spend your Thursday afternoon in a bubble bath reading a book, it doesn't matter what they think!

So how is your ability to self-nurture? Are you bound by rules of learnt behaviour from your upbringing and/or culture? Have you found a balance that works for you? This isn't just about health care in the traditional sense. Self-nurture can extend to ensuring your interests are met too. Most life coaches encourage their clients to take time for themselves in their week in order to address their own needs. Some, like the wonderfully practical Cheryl Richardson, encourage their clients to make a date with themselves once a week. This is taking a part of one day a week, either a morning, an afternoon or an evening, as a sacred space for yourself which is not postponed or changed due to others' needs or your inability to prioritise. It is essentially a date with yourself. She recommends if possible that you use the same time every week as this tends to instil the habit. You choose what to do on that date each time: Have a bubble bath; visit a museum; listen to music; go hiking; go out to dinner; go window shopping; snuggle on the sofa with a movie or, whatever you choose. The important thing is that you are consciously taking the time to nurture yourself once a week in an act of self-love, and you ring fence it in your diary, because you are important.

Below is some space to write down some ideas that you have about self-nurturing.

Exercise: *Planning Self-Nurturing Time and Activities*

What do I Really Like Doing to Relax? When Can I Prioritise This?

Number Five in my top tips to being your Authentic Self and Loving Yourself: **Knowing What You Are Here For.**

Some of us find it hard to love ourselves because we don't know, or we don't think we know, what we are here for – and we think we should. Some of us feel there is a reason why we are here, but we don't know what it is, and that the longer we can't work it out, the more we are wasting time. Or we may recognise that we do have a feeling of what we are here to do and achieve, but we cannot seem to get there or find a way of doing so. Others of us may feel we aren't here for any reason and that everyone else is more important because they do appear to live a life of purpose.

One thing I am sure of is that we are all here to learn. That learning whatever it is, forms part of our purpose. Some of us have definitely decided to come here with a big mission in mind whilst others of us are here to relax a bit more. I have three children and one of them is full of angst as they feel they have so much to do and so little time, one of them is firmly convinced that they are here to have fun and the other is somewhere in the middle! I believe that our purpose is whatever we chose, whatever we sub-consciously or consciously decide, and we can choose if we do it and we can change it if we want to do something different.

Sometimes we cannot even think straight to even ask ourselves what we enjoy doing or what we would like to be doing, let alone the age-old question *'What am I here for?'* Sometimes we have so much stuff draining us in our lives that we lack the energy to tackle everyday tasks, let alone think about saving the world, creating the next best business success or inventing a machine that will save lives. So, what is draining *you*? Think about areas in your life such as your home, work, romantic relationship, family, your health, friendships and your involvement in your community.

Identifying the 'drains' in your life is a great start. Now you can choose to allow them to keep on draining you, and draining your ability to Becoming Love™, or you can take one of the things from your list every day, each week, each month, or whenever you plan to, and plug those drains with self-loving action by taking charge of yourself. It is amazing how completing and then maintaining just one of these items from the lists will brighten your day and leave you feeling more positive about the bigger picture in your life. Without day to day life feeling so exhausting, is it possible to think about what you would really like to be doing? What is your purpose?

Whatever you are here to learn and whether you have a purpose that you would like to be living, it can be a relief to realise and accept it; knowing it is always your choice and you can choose to do it or change it whenever you like. Some of the people I work with have fears surrounding their 'purpose' or their 'soul purpose.' They may be afraid they will never realise what it is and so 'fail their mission'. Or that if they are not quick, someone will take their idea which is their purpose and realise the potential of it before they do. They fear it will be snatched from their grasp. This possible failure creates jealousy, disappointment or fears about punishment and criticism.

My feeling is that, as amazing beings with free will, we choose what we came here to learn, so ultimately our purpose is our own... it is ours and ours alone. No one can take it from you. There is not a room full of 'helium balloon purposes' floating around above our heads which us mere mortals must jump for and grab and try to hold onto for the rest of our lives. Rather they are uninflated balloons that we already have. All you have to do is put your hand in your pocket, pull out one of the uninflated balloons in your own pocket and start blowing into it. Start living your purpose and creating your life, your way. It is *your* purpose. *You* create it and only *you* can. If you complete it, or you want a different one, put your hand in your pocket and pull out another. It really is as simple as that.

There is no need to stress about finding your purpose (running around jumping and trying to grab a spare balloon), you already know it, the balloon is already in your pocket as a germ of an idea, waiting for you to blow life into it if you want to. There is no pressure. Your life and what you do with it is your choice. So, relax and do what you enjoy. Why would you choose a purpose that is no fun for you? If you take time to study successful people, you will notice those who are most happy are the ones who are doing what they love. They are living their purpose. They know that their passion is their power. Successful people are very often doing exactly what they love doing. Whether that is cooking like Jamie Oliver, acting like Jennifer Aniston, or working within the industry you love, like Yvon Chouinard, an avid climber who founded Patagonia, an outdoor clothing company.

All these people will tell you that they knew what they wanted to do and what drove them. They knew what their passion was. Their success was a result of them following their passion and believing in themselves and what they were doing. The success was a by-product of them following their passions. Even people who are not famous can usually attribute their success to doing what they love and are good at: fund managers love moving money around and taking risks; surgeons love to fix the human body with their skilled hands and pilots love to fly planes. Those who follow their passions find success.

Of course, there will always be exceptions to the rule. Many financially abundant people find their work highly stressful but, if a person is earning a lot of money but hates their job which takes all of their time, are they successful? I don't consider them successful because they are not happy, and this is inevitably going to affect their family life, their relationships and their health. For me success is an abundance of all things desirable: happiness; love; health, personal growth and of course, money. *You* deserve happiness, success, health, financial abundance, love and spiritual growth. Don't you? Are you ready to have it all?

Take some time to think about what you love doing and what you are good at. This could be indicated by what you do in your spare time, what books you like to read, what you feel your life's purpose is or something you do in your daily life that you really enjoy. It could even be something you always mean to make time to do but don't often get around to. Think also about what aspects of your life you feel confident and most at ease in. Make a list of all of these things that come to mind in the space below.

Exercise: *What am I here for?*

What am I passionate about?	What am I good at?	In what areas of my life do I feel most confident?	Where do the lists correlate? This is your starting point!

When you take a look at some of the things you have written down, do any fit with ideas you have already had? Perhaps you have noticed yourself pulled in this direction or have seen 'signs' or had opportunities but just didn't take them or recognise them at the time. Take time to formulate some ideas around this direction for yourself. This will lead you to an initial plan of action if your purpose is something you are wanting to actively engage in. It may be on a voluntary basis, a career, or a personal goal. You don't have to know everything before you start. You just have to start and allow things to unfold, be open minded and follow the power of your passion to find your purpose.

Remember it could be one thing or a number of things. It could be to spread joy to old people or play music to millions. It could be to have fun and joy every day or to work with orphans in Ghana. No one purpose has a higher value than another. It is not about any others who may benefit, it is about you doing what you want to do. My only directive is this, if you feel that you were somehow sent here as the 'only one' who can save the world or bring a message, then it could be your ego talking over your inner wisdom! There is space below to write down some of your ideas and plans.

Exercise: *How Can I Start to Live my Purpose?*

My thoughts and plans for living my purpose.

Number six in my top tips to being your Authentic Self and Loving Yourself: **Being in Balance**

Having balance in your life, on a daily basis, and over a week, over a month and indeed annually, means that you create time to work, rest and play in the right amounts for you. Having this kind of lifestyle balance allows you to breathe and to feel that there is always enough time. It allows and encourages you to make more time for yourself and others, and ensures that you have enough energy. It is not a new philosophy and most life coaches encourage their clients to find this equilibrium as a starting point or in conjunction with whatever else it is they are trying to achieve. It is a very popular theory and for good reason; studies have shown if you have balance in your life, you will function at a higher level of productivity, you will be happier and healthier.

As the world becomes more technologically advanced, life becomes faster paced and we can become caught up in the whirlwind of 'existing'. We live our lives by going with the flow and we can get stuck in the grooves of day to day tasks. We find ourselves making plans which include the words, *'It will be ok when…',* or, *'I'll start doing that after…',* or even, *'I'll just get this out of the way, then …'*

Creating balance in your life requires you to stop 'firefighting' your way through life and ask yourself *'When?'* When will you start living and being the driver of your own life? Taking back control and steering yourself in the direction you want to go now is the key. Organising your home and finances, focussing your energy on maintaining your health, and getting in touch with your inner self are all important in the process. Having a balance in your life between work, fun, fostering relationships, emotional and physical health, is important to actually *living*, rather than just *existing*.

There are many variations in the concept of what is the ideal balance for anyone, and different life coaches and mentors may recommend slightly different 'ideal lifestyle balances' and how to create this practically. So, I recommend that you do a little research, perhaps online or by browsing in bookshops or your local library, to find a balance theory that suits you. There is a wealth of information about this on the internet and in books, so you can find some advice on the type of balance that resonates with you and start to create that balance in your life. It is not always easy to do this, particularly if you are already leading a busy life where it already feels that there is never enough time without adding in all these extra 'time slots'. However, it is easy to find excuses, and the truth is we are all responsible for ourselves and our lives. Nobody is truly stuck, there are always choices; the decisions may be very difficult to make, but there will be options.

Thinking about creating balance in your life may feel easy, but it is assumed that acting is trickier. Does it have to be? Small steps can make a huge inroad toward the freedom of living life the way you want to. You can start by readdressing small imbalances. Make those changes and soon they become habits; when you are comfortable then you can make further changes. It is also easier to address balance in your overall life by making changes to your home and work space so they reflect your needs. For example, if your home is not a peaceful, nurturing space in which you feel comfortable, begin by de-cluttering and rearranging small areas of rooms at a time.

Getting in touch with your true self and improving your mental, physical and emotional health, must work alongside such practical steps, to ensure you know what you really want and have the energy to go after it. There are a thousand and one ways of doing this and many of them are all free! Make time in your week to take a date with yourself doing something very simple and freeing. You could lose yourself in some music, walk in the park, read a good library book wrapped up in a duvet. You could take yourself out of your comfort zone on a regular basis and try something new, or have a good cry and a good laugh at a film. Remember when running down a hill yelling with your arms outstretched felt like fun? It still is! In whichever way you choose to address the concept of balance in your life, the more you feel you are in the 'right' balance for you, the more you are choosing to love yourself. The more you can love yourself, the more you can love others, and of course the more they will love you because you will invite it and allow it.

Below are some beliefs or programmes that you may have which could be holding you back from finding balance in your life. In Chapter 1 of this book you will find some information on how to test for beliefs that you consciously or subconsciously have. Test the beliefs below now to see if you have any of these programmes.

Exercise: *Testing for beliefs about being in balance*

Stand up and test the beliefs below, as shown in Chapter 1. Remember to ensure that you are testing *YES/NO* correctly before you start, to speak aloud and to have your eyes closed.

	Belief to Check	Desired Response	Your check mark*
1	It is wrong to be self-full	No	
2	It is good to be selfless	No	
3	I am selfish.	No	
4	If I love myself I will become arrogant.	No	
5	If I love myself I will have too much fun and forget what I came here to do.	No	
6	Selflessness is a virtue.	No	
7	I have to help everyone who asks me.	No	
8	I always put others' needs first.	No	
9	I am a martyr.	No	
10	I have to be a martyr.	No	
11	I love my body	Yes	
12	I love my mind.	Yes	
13	I love my soul.	Yes	
14	I know what it feels like to love myself.	Yes	
15	I do love myself.	Yes	

Remember, by the time you have finished working through this book, you may find that some of these belief programmes have changed to the 'desired response' by your learning, self-recognition, and taking positive action towards Becoming Love™. So, do not worry if you feel you have all of these programmes now; you are a beautiful work in progress and already perfect.

Number Seven in my top tips to being your Authentic Self and Loving Yourself: **Self- Acceptance**

Self-acceptance requires you to be truly honest with yourself, to recognise your motives, your inner most desires and fears, to recognise your strengths and weaknesses, and to accept yourself knowing you can change if you choose to. Self-acceptance leads to self-love. Loving yourself as you are now, as you have been and as you will be; self-acceptance understands the authentic you in all your glory as a beautiful work in progress. Self-acceptance demands the practices of self-forgiveness, responsibility and accountability; it is a loving, strong feeling.

When was the last time you made a major decision without talking it through with someone else? External validation can be a great thing; it is a really useful tool to help us take major life changing moves. Advice from friends, experts and family at important times in our lives is wonderful. However, it is when the balance tips from having this type of support on hand, to *needing* external validation for our normal day to day lives that there may be a problem. If we are seeking validation from others on a day to day basis, then it is an indication that we are lacking in self-acceptance. Requiring others to tell us we 'look great today' or we are socially acceptable, by posting a selfie on Instagram regularly and often, could be considered an extreme version of this need. This practice of so called 'propaganda selfies' has become so much a part of our everyday life, that it is considered normal amongst teenagers to value themselves on the number of 'likes' they get on social media – even if they buy them themselves!

When did you stop trusting yourself to decide for yourself if you were wearing the right clothes, making the right choices or hanging out in the right places? I have lovely memories of my oldest daughter when she was a toddler wearing a tutu and wellies every day and everywhere she went. She knew looked exactly how she wanted to and it was the perfect outfit for every occasion. She didn't care that it wasn't in fashion or that it wasn't 'normal' attire for walking the dog. She wasn't choosing her outfit to make a statement or to fit in, she wore what she liked because she liked it.

The more you learn to accept yourself, the more you are able to trust yourself to make your own choices and daily decisions without needing external validation. To do what you think is right without having to 'shout' about it is the key to self-validation. Would you like to know you are worthy of doing this, that you know how to accept yourself without requiring external validation, and it is possible for you?

Often, those of us who lack some self-acceptance tend to also be procrastinators or perfectionists. In one way both of these attributes achieve the same goal. Both being a perfectionist or a procrastinator allows you to put off completing something. It allows you the 'freedom' to push away what you really want to do, perhaps because you are afraid to move forward. Fear is a lack of love so what you really need is more self-love. There is no need to be completely self-accepting to love yourself. There is no need to wait until you have lost weight, found your soul mate, finished your education, completed your life's mission or anything else before you can love yourself. It is a journey of discovery not an end point. Living in the moment, recognising where you are and where you are going and accepting yourself as you are, as you were and as you will be, will lead you to self-reverence.

Self-acceptance leads to more confidence, in the true sense of the word. How do you know when someone is really self-accepting and at peace with themselves or just really good at 'faking it until they make it'? Some of the most socially outgoing people I know have very low esteem and will be the first to admit that they are very good at putting on a brave face, shrugging life off with self-effacing humour, or by poking fun at others.

Real confidence comes from within, from a position of self-acceptance and self-love. It is not always possible to measure another's confidence from their popularity, their social behaviour, their appearance or what others say about them. Confidence doesn't have to shout or be surrounded by crowds; it is a calm, sense of inner knowing and self-recognition.

Truly confident people know their own strengths and weaknesses. They offer support to others and allow themselves to receive support when they need it. They accept themselves and recognise that if they make a mistake they can take responsibility for it, can learn from it and move forward without having to hold onto guilt or shame. They know their own mind without having to impose their beliefs on others, and they allow others to have their own opinions, without having to agree with them.

Some people are born with this self-esteem whereas most of us learn it as we go along. There are simple affirmations that can help. Telling yourself daily that your opinion matters, that you are worthy of recognition and that you have something to offer can help. Other people find it useful to make a list of all the ways in which they do feel confident and then another of the ways in which they are yet to feel fully confident. Assessing what they would need to do in order to feel more confident in these areas is a useful exercise to moving towards better self-esteem. Recognising that you have skills in some areas and not yet in others, but that is okay, is a way to feel self-acceptance. Confidence isn't about being good at everything – it is about accepting the way you are now and recognising you can choose to reach a higher potential.

The next exercise is designed to assist you in acquiring certain feelings which will help you to Become Love by learning to accept and love yourself. Firstly, take a pen and read the statements of feelings below. Circle YES to any of them that you would like to feel or think you already do feel. The second part of this exercise is to make yourself comfortable and listen to the *track 6*, a meditation entitled, **Allow Yourself to Receive Gifts**, on the **Becoming Love™ Meditation Album**. All of these feelings below are included on the *track 6, **Allow Yourself to Receive Gifts Meditation*** which you can listen to and enjoy now, later and as many times as you like. So, first, read the feeling statements and circle YES if you feel this already or would like to feel this.

Exercise: *Feeling work on Self-Acceptance*

Feelings You Already Have or Would Like to Have	Circle the word YES if you would like to have this feeling or feel you already do have it.
Would you like to already know how to and what it feels like to see yourself as you truly are?	YES
Would you like to already know how to and what it feels like to hear yourself as you truly are?	YES
Would you like to already know how to and what it feels like to know yourself as you truly are?	YES
Would you like to already know how to and what it feels like to listen to yourself as you deserve to be listened to?	YES
Would you like to already know how to and what it feels like to accept yourself as you deserve to be accepted?	YES
Would you like to already know how to and what it feels like to love yourself as you truly are?	YES
Would you like to already know how to and what it feels like to revere yourself as you truly are?	YES
Would you like to already know how to and what it feels like to have compassion for yourself?	YES

Would you like to already know how to and what it feels like to be kind to yourself as you truly deserve?	YES
Would you like to already know how to and what it feels like to nurture yourself as you truly deserve?	YES
Would you like to already know how to and what it feels like to respect yourself as you truly deserve?	YES
Would you like to already know how to and what it feels like to love yourself unconditionally as you truly deserve to be loved?	YES

Meditation: *Allow Yourself to Receive Gifts*

Now listen to the **Becoming Love™ Meditation Album,** *track 6, Allow Yourself to Receive Gifts,* which will assist you to process these feelings that you have circled above, and to feel self-acceptance by showing yourself love. All you have to do is to listen and be guided by my voice.

> Make yourself comfortable in a quiet place where you will not be disturbed for about 30 minutes. You could sit or lie down. Now, listen to the ***Allow Yourself to Receive Gifts Meditation*** which is *track 6,* on the **Becoming Love™ Meditation Album.**
>
> All of the feelings in the exercise above are included on this meditation; as you listen to it, you can just allow the sound of my voice to wash over you and relax. You don't need to respond if you hear me asking you a question because by completing the questions above you have already made your intentions clear, but if you choose to affirm or not in your head, you can do so.
>
> If you find you lose track of what I am saying, don't worry, just allow yourself to sense whatever comes to you. Afterwards you may like to write your experience down so you remember the 'gifts' you were given; there is space to do that.
>
> Relax and enjoy now!

Exercise: *Gifts I was Given in my Meditation*

You can note down your meditation experience in the box below.

Gifts I Felt I Received in my Meditation Experience

Allowing yourself to receive is a good way to feel self-acceptance and you can listen to this meditation again later and as many times as you like. You will find you experience something slightly different each time and, as you get used to allowing yourself to reach this deep meditative state, you will find your experiences become more profound.

Now you have addressed loving yourself more, we are going to take a look at your amazing heart and soul, and the potential you have to love; to help you experience loving others better and in doing so, Becoming Love™.

CHAPTER 5

Delving into the Heart and Soul

As we begin to love ourselves more, it is easier to love others. This section begins with a short exercise which focusses on seeing others from a higher level of understanding. It is from this perspective that we can begin to feel agape or reverence for humanity. Seeing others from this higher understanding will allow you to revere all others in our wonderful human network.

Many of us are so overwhelmed with how we are perceived by others, that we are unable to really see them. If we lack confidence, we may assume other's remarks are criticising us. How many times has someone said to you *'I didn't mean it like that.'* Some of us are resentful of others, perhaps due to a personal experience, and we allow that resentment to extend to a group of people who remind us of that one person, that one situation where we were hurt. So, we form prejudices without realising it, to keep us safe from being hurt again; we form a resentment towards anyone who reminds us of that painful time, and so going forward we dislike, judge or criticise anyone who falls into this group. Many of us make subconscious assumptions about groups of people based on these original resentments towards one person. Sometimes these assumptions are based on what is generally assumed by our community. Despite popular belief, not all 'yummy mummies' have happy marriages, not all rich people are arrogant, and not all Guardian readers are champagne socialists......do you get the picture...?

Heart

In order to start seeing others in this new way, as unique individuals who are learning just like we are, it helps if we can release hurt, pain, sorrow, resentments and feelings of being judged or criticised, that we are still holding onto. As we release the negative feelings, it makes more room for the love to come in. Imagine your heart being like a vessel. If it is full of negative feelings and memories there is no room for the good stuff, so by letting them go we automatically make room for new, positive feelings. The next meditation, *track 7,* is designed to help you do this. It will guide you through a heart clearing and is an interactive exercise designed to free your heart of these negative emotions that are no longer serving you.

Meditation: *Heart Clearing*

As with all of the meditations included in Becoming Love™, you can revisit them as many times as you like but this interactive meditative exercise is one I particularly recommend doing on a regular basis. It is extremely cathartic and once you have followed my guidance a few times you will probably find you can do it without the **Becoming Love™ Meditation Album** to guide you. There is space to write down what you experience below, if you would like to.

When you listen to the meditation you will hear my voice guiding you into a deep meditative state and you will be asked to imagine you are inside your own heart. You will be invited to imagine negative feelings such as sorrow leaving your heart and to use your hands to gently tap over your heart space to help the release.

As you do so, you may find that after a while, you become conscious of memories or old, forgotten feelings. If you do, that is great. Allow it. Keep breathing as guided and allow those emotions, feelings and memories to come up and be released. You may find you cry, that's perfectly normal too. Don't be tempted to wipe tears away, just allow them to fall.

The important thing is to keep breathing, tapping and keep imagining you are inside your heart. You may hear my voice reminding you to do this but likewise you may be so deep into your meditation that you are unaware of me; either way is fine. There is plenty of time to release and then you will hear me guide you back into your own space again.

Some people find it hard to relax into at first so you may need to do it a few times until you feel it is really working for you. If you found you were just in your stride and then my voice guided you to stop, you can repeat and next time just finish when you are ready. The most important thing is to make this a personal experience for you.

Make yourself comfortable in a quiet place where you will not be disturbed for about 30 minutes. You could sit or lie down. Now, listen to the ***Heart Clearing Meditation*** which is *track 7,* on the **Becoming Love™ Meditation Album.**

Relax and enjoy now!

Exercise: *My Experience of the Heart Clearing Meditation*

Write down anything you would like to recall about your experiences of the meditation in the box below, if you wish to.

During the heart clearing meditation, I felt...

The more your own heart is clear of past hurt, sorrow, resentments and sadness, the easier it is to start to see people as individuals who have their own paths, likes, dislikes, strengths and weaknesses. We are all here trying to work things out in our own way. Is it possible for you to see this truth in others?

Many of us find it very difficult to love humanity, for lots of different reasons, and so the following exercise is designed to assist you in acquiring certain feelings which will help you to Become Love by seeing others from a higher level of understanding, without getting caught up in judgement, criticism or taking on their 'stuff' as your own. Wouldn't it be wonderful if we could look straight through someone straight into their hearts and really see them? If we could see their fears, their desires and their motives? It would reveal what they are really like. We could really see them from the highest perspective, and love them.

Exercise: *Seeing and Loving Others*

Firstly, take a pen and read the statements of feelings below. Circle YES to any of them that you would like to feel or think you already do feel this. The second part of this exercise is to make yourself comfortable and listen to the *track 8*, on the **Becoming Love™ Meditation Album**. All of these feelings below are included on *track 8*, **Seeing and Loving Others** which you can listen to and enjoy now, later and as many times as you like.

Feelings for Seeing and Loving Others

Feelings You Already Have or Would Like to Have	Circle the word YES if you would like to have this feeling or feel you already do have it.
Would you like to be able to see others as they truly are and know what it feels like to do so?	YES
Would you like to be able to hear others as they truly are and know what it feels like to do so?	YES
Would you like to be able to accept others as they truly are and know what it feels like to do so?	YES
Would you like to be able to love others as they truly are and know what it feels like to do so?	YES
Would you like to be able to love others as they truly are and know what it feels like to do so?	YES
Would you like to understand others' points of view without having to…?	
… agree with them	YES
… fight with them	YES
… justify yourself to them	YES
… feel stupid	YES
… feel attacked	YES
Would you like to know how to allow others to learn in the way that they choose to learn?	YES

Meditation: *Seeing and Loving Others*

> Make yourself comfortable in a quiet place where you will not be disturbed for about 30 minutes. You could sit or lie down.
>
> Now, listen to the **Seeing and Loving Others Meditation** which is *track 8,* on the **Becoming Love™ Meditation Album.**
>
> All of the feelings in the exercise above are included on this meditation; as you listen to it, you can just allow the sound of my voice to wash over you and relax. You don't need to respond if you hear me asking you a question because by completing the questions above you have already made your intentions clear, but if you choose to affirm or not in your head, you can do so.
>
> If you find you lose track of what I am saying, don't worry, just allow yourself to sense whatever comes to you. Just allow the feeling of love and acceptance for others flow through you and around you.
>
> Relax and enjoy now!

Soul

When you can feel another's heart and their truth, then loving them is easy. If we could see their soul, the essence of them, their spirit, their mojo, whatever you label it - if you could, just for a second - imagine what you could feel for them. We are all amazing souls in human bodies, living human lives and learning as we go. I believe our souls chose to do this and however hard we think life is at times, I have a sneaky suspicion that our souls are having a great time! I like to think of our souls as the essence of us from all time and between time, and that right now we are living within our human bodies. Whatever you believe, just imagine when I talk of the soul that I am talking about the essence of each of us. Feeling and seeing our own and others' heart and their soul and their truth is refreshing and supports you in Becoming Love™.

If you feel in tune with people and with their souls as you interact with them on a daily basis, you will love them and they will feel it. Souls are beautiful. Many people paint souls to highlight their incredible power and allure. My wonderful friend, Nancy Green, who created the cover for this book, is an expert at this. If you are a creative person you can paint a soul, sing a soul, dance a soul, or describe it poetically. Souls can be revealed and entertained by beauty, mystery and love. Creatives have been doing this for centuries through music, poetry and works of art. The most popular music is that which stirs our souls and has been played all over the world for years and years. Likewise, certain works of art have become icons due to their soul captivating quality; people will stand and stare at some paintings for a long time because they are so powerful and intriguing.

To 'see' someone's soul you need only look. This sounds simple, and it is. When I look into someone's soul, I see colours and shapes, all converging like a kaleidoscope making exquisite patterns. Some may hear its beautiful song. You may feel its power and glory. You may have a sense of knowing what that soul is capable of. By following the next meditation, you are going to experience your own soul so you can really appreciate your magnitude. You will really see how amazing your own soul is. All of you have the most amazing souls and once you have experienced yours, you will have a greater understanding of the essence of every other person on our planet. We are all amazing souls. In whatever way you 'witness' during the meditation, whether you see it in your mind's eye, feel it, get a sense of knowing or hear it, that experience is perfect. You may find the more you use these meditations that your sensory experiences change as your intuition develops; it often happens that the more we open our minds to explore in this meditative way, the more we develop our intuitive senses. Are you ready?

Meditation: *Soul Scanning*

When you have listened to this guided meditation you may like to draw what you saw or felt, or perhaps make some notes in the space provided below. Be prepared to love the essence of you and in doing so realising how easy it is to love the essence of all humanity.

> When you listen to the meditation you will hear my voice guiding you into a deep meditative state. You may hear my voice guiding you throughout but you may be so deep into your meditation that you are unaware of me; either way is fine. There is plenty of time to scan your soul in whatever way that comes to you, and then you will hear me guide you back into your own space again. Just allow the sound of my voice to wash over you and relax. You don't need to respond if you hear me asking you a question, but if you choose to, you can do so. If you find you lose track of what I am saying, don't worry, just allow yourself to sense whatever comes to you.
>
> Some people find it hard to relax into at first, so you may need to do it a few times until you feel it is really working for you. If you found you were just in your stride and then my voice guided you to stop, you can repeat and next time just finish when you are ready. The most important thing is to make this a personal experience for you.
>
> Make yourself comfortable in a quiet place where you will not be disturbed for about 30 minutes. You could sit or lie down. Now, listen to the ***Soul Scanning Meditation*** which is *track 9*, on the **Becoming Love™ Meditation Album.**
>
> Relax and enjoy now!

Exercise: *Experiences of Soul Scanning Meditation*

Use the space below to draw or write how you sensed your soul during the Soul Scanning Meditation.

During the meditation, I saw, felt, experienced or sensed that my soul was……..

This chapter has really allowed you to think about your hearts and souls, so I am going to finish this section with a question for you. What would happen if you really let someone see you? What would it feel like to really let someone see your heart? Are you brave enough to let someone see your soul, to really know the essence of you? If you allowed others to really see you, what would that feel like? Does it feel threatening? Does it make you feel weak or vulnerable? Does it feel frightening? Do you feel people would start walking all over you?

It is a common misconception that we have to hide our real selves so we stay safe but hiding means you are never safe. If you spend your whole life hiding, not only are you coming from a state of fear, cowering out of sight behind a wall or a shield, you are also never allowing yourself to really step into yourself and enjoy life. If you are hiding, you are in a constant state of fear on some level and, if you are fearful, you are not moving forward on an energetic level.

Are you in a state of fear? When animals are frightened for themselves or their young ones, they either run away or they attack. Do you run away or are you always ready to defend yourself? Or perhaps you are always alert and more likely to attack? Is being aggressive or 'striking first' your way of surviving?

If you feel you hide yourself for any reason, you are limiting yourself to only *some* love. How can your family or partner love you completely and unconditionally if you do not reveal all of yourself? How can you love others completely and unconditionally if you only allow a part of yourself out there into the world to do the loving? Many of us have fears around being vulnerable if we are truly open, but of course you can have discernment. Just because you are being you and true to yourself, doesn't mean you automatically lose all sense of discernment. You can still know who to trust and when, how to communicate in the most appropriate way, with the right words in the right situation.

Allowing yourself to be seen and loved for who you are is empowering. When you feel loved and empowered, it is easy to love others. You can be patient while others explain what they want to say, and you can really hear them in the way they intend to be heard. You can also really hear their unconscious intentions too, without taking offence or judging them. Imagine this example:

I was working away and attending some seminars, and had booked a massage with a guy who gives phenomenal massages based on Thai style but with his own twist. A colleague who I had come to know pretty well over the weeks saw his arrival at my place and said, 'I'm so glad you felt able to treat yourself to a massage. Lucky you! He charges such a lot! You must feel you deserve it!' This comment at face value is fine but what she was also saying without words was: 'Poor me! I cannot afford a massage. You are so lucky and don't know it. Spending all those dollars on a massage is frivolous. Why can't I have one? You should feel guilty.'

I heard her words and I heard all of her subconscious intent. Maybe a number of years ago I would have felt guilty or embarrassed and defended my decision to buy a massage, or I might have made some smart remark back because I felt attacked. But I saw her heart and her soul, and heard her and felt nothing but reverence. I felt how much I had shifted. You might say that by noticing or 'hearing' her intent that I was caught up in my own feelings and judging her. You may think that if I was truly coming from love, I would have taken her words at face value. That is not how it works; Becoming Love™ doesn't mean you become stupid or unable to read people. It does not mean you are weak or naïve. It doesn't mean you stop becoming intuitive. Actually, in my experience, you see clearer than ever, but you don't feel angry or upset, insulted or hurt, defensive or attacked; you feel love.

It is not a question of letting people get one up on you. This is the common misinterpretation of the message in 'turning the other cheek'. Coming from love and loving others means you are equipped with the strongest emotion on the planet. If you love people, whether the meaning behind their words is conscious or unconscious, you are always ready with reverence and agape. There are no winners or losers; there is only love. I believe that the concept of 'turning the other cheek' is about communicating with others with love. It encourages us to understand the other person's needs and accept them, without diminishing ourselves or allowing others to take advantage of us. It is not an ego driven energy of being *so* enlightened that you can allow others to 'misbehave' without rising to annoyance; it is honest and humble. It is an energy of Becoming Love™.

CHAPTER 6

Learning Love from Others

Learning from our Families and our Ancestors

All of us have good and bad relationships with different members of our family. We may know stories of how wonderful or how tyrannical some members of our family were, even the ones that we never got the chance to meet. I believe we can learn a lot of good from our families and ancestors, particularly if we take the time to consider their qualities. I have explored some of my ancestors' lives and their mastering of reverence. I wanted to learn more about showing reverence for humanity through their knowledge and wisdom.

I have an ancestor who was a teacher in a boarding school for young boys in England. He had been a writer and a journalist, and once retired, taught art to the young boys at the school. He really loved them and knew that, being so young and away from home, sometimes they felt lonely or unsure. He taught them how to express themselves through drawing and creative work. He encouraged, he motivated and he loved. He spent time with them in the grounds of the school showing them the art and beauty in nature and how to see the wonder in the universe. He showed them how to feel at one with their environment, so they never felt alone. I'm told that he seemed to have the knack of just knowing when a small boy was feeling especially lonely and he would seek him out and chat to him, show him a magic trick and listen to him. He would restore their energy so they could run back to their friends and throw themselves back into school life. He was a marvellous man. From finding out about him I learnt how to sense when people needed love, and how to support them in a small every day way; a smile; a quick chat; a hug; a telephone call; a small gift or an invitation. These little acts of humanity help people feel loved and special and we can all do that every day in small ways with the people we interact with.

Within my immediate family of my parents, my siblings and my children, I can see that they all have different virtues of love. By observing them and collating all the best bits I can learn from them too. Of course, as happens in all families, they all also drive me crazy in their own way too, as I have no doubt I do them, but I can recognise the wonderful ways they embrace love and learn that aspect for myself. My mother is incredibly generous with her time, energy and resources. My oldest daughter is one of the most forgiving people I know. My sister loves her children with a fierce and proud love whilst being completely aware of all of their strengths and weaknesses at the same time. My son continues to go on loving without response because he knows that loving is a strength, and my youngest daughter is so accomplished at self-love that she stands in her own power and radiates sunshine with equal measures of practical wisdom well in advance of her teenage years.

Exercise: *Aspects of Love my Family has Mastered and What I can Learn from Them.*

How about your family? Below is a space to record what aspects of love you can identify that your family have mastered. Recognising and acknowledging this will assist you in taking on that quality too.

Name			
Aspect of Love			
Name			
Aspect of Love			
Name			
Aspect of Love			

Nicola van Dyke

Learning From 'Masters'

Whether you are affiliated to one religion or none, regardless of your culture or your environment, most of us can agree that there have been some pretty awesome humans over the last few thousands of years, in terms of their ability to love. We may not all resonate with the same ones, or even acknowledge all of their actual existence in the way they are recorded, but most of us can recall one or two figures in the history of the world who seemed to have a good handle on the concept of love and reverence for humanity. These humans appear to have mastered many virtues and understood how to love others; they were known for showing it through their words and actions. Some of them it appears learnt how to do it through their own lifetime experiences, whilst others appear to have shown up on this beautiful planet of ours all set to go. Some people refer to these enlightened human beings, as masters because they have 'mastered' many virtues.

Arguably the greatest of all the virtues that can be mastered is love, because it is all encompassing, and at the core of love in all its complexity is reverence. I think we can learn a lot from these masters about reverence for humanity. I am not suggesting that everything recorded about these people is all true but there will be some of these masters' ideas that resonate with you, and it is possible to take ideas and learn from their wisdom. There is much to learn from so many, and we all interpret what we read and learn in our own way. So, forgive me if what I share does not meet your understanding or interpretation.

When thinking about peace in the world, I came across some teachings by a learned master from over a thousand years ago. I found his words very gentle, peaceful and loving. They described the effect of a pebble being dropped into the middle of a huge lake of calm water. Even though the lake may be very big, and

Becoming Love™

the pebble very small, the ripples from it entering the water spread out so far that they touched the edges of the shore. One small act of human love can ripple out and not only affect one person or situation, but also influence others in a way that we don't even realise or recognise at that time. We can positively affect people in ways that we don't perceive or predict at the time. If one person with one small act of reverence once can create this ripple of love, imagine what one small act every day by one person can do. Imagine what all of us doing one small act a day could do! What if we all stepped up and committed to two or three small acts of love every day? By one small action, one small act of love, we as individuals can begin to spread love throughout humanity. And of course, if all of us individuals do it, then imagine how those ripples of love spread across the world.

My passion is reverence and love for others, so I am of course interested in what many of the religious masters teach. Jesus appears to have been a great man with human needs and emotions who channelled love in every essence of his being. He demonstrated reverence for humanity on a practical level. By reading about his life and behaviour toward others, we can realise how through our everyday actions and also through specific projects, we can Become Love. We can not only feel love but we can show others how to. Love isn't just a state of mind, it is a way of behaving towards others and towards yourself. We are humans. We feel anger and sadness; it is part of our nature, but it is how you choose to express these emotions and how you communicate them that is important.

When I think of Siddhārtha Gautama at the end of his life, he feels like compassion personified. His teachings show us how to love others as an energy of stillness. He demonstrates how to stand back with compassion, seeing and allowing others to be as they truly are, reacting with kindness, peace and acceptance.

Through his teachings we can learn to stand in our own power of agape, observe and allow. When studying the teaching of Guru Nanak, the founder of Sikhism, the messages of love are clear. We can all love and, how we choose to show others or demonstrate, it must be comfortable for us. We should love in our own way that makes ourselves and others feel relaxed. Other Sikh Gurus have further wisdom. Guru Gobind Singh's teachings remind us that we all have strengths and weaknesses. We can show love for others by being strong where they are weak and allowing their strength to support us when we are weak. We can all support others and receive support without shame or being superior.

There are so many words of wisdom from so many masters and these examples are just a few that resonated with me. You may be inspired by others' teachings about love and enjoy applying the ideas in your day to day life. There is a whole world out there of people who need to experience feeling loved completely for who they are, and likewise being shown how to love. There are many of us who feel it is important or even part of our purpose to do this and you can only follow your heart and do it your way. Go where you feel you want to go, and when you want to go and show love for others in your own unique way.

Most of the amazing humans from whom we can learn reverence were not religious leaders or founders, they were ordinary people with extraordinary vision. In seeking some inspiration on love, I came across some ancient teachings on the practice of yoga. I have always meant to take up this exercise routine regularly and one day I really will! I found the words really resonated with me. The messages were full of joy and inner dance. They instilled that to love others you have to know inner joy and allow yourself to dance – metaphorically! They encouraged that by experiencing this joy of self, this inner wonder and self-love of your own body, your own mind and soul, that you can then love others easily.

Through the teachings of Rumi, an early thirteenth century Persian poet, we can learn that love is everywhere. It is in every person, every animal and every living being in every corner of our world. We can choose to notice it, find it, harness it and experience it and by doing so we can share it with others.

> **'Stop acting so small. You are the universe in ecstatic motion.'**
>
> *Rumi*

It is widely thought that Mother Theresa selflessly devoted her time and energy to others and I was fascinated to learn her philosophy on self-love, as it would appear at first glance at her life, that she was selfless and not one for practising self-fullness. She spoke once about how there would always be others to help, like a never-ending queue of people waiting for love. So, if you were choosing to support them, you need to find time to nurture yourself with peace, rest, food, and self-love, in order that you approach every person who comes to you with patience, kindness and complete focus. The people needing love will keep on coming, there is no foreseeable end. You cannot attend to yourself when you have finished supporting them all as there will always be more people to support. You must take your time when you need it, so you are better placed to attend to those who need you. This is an excellent way to explain the necessity for self-fullness.

There is a so much wisdom from so many 'masters' who can support you in Becoming Love™; some you may know the name of already and some you won't. Some are well known or famous, others are just ordinary people going about their ordinary lives doing and saying extraordinary things. There are examples of people showing love to others in amazing ways all over the world every day. The messages they have for you are specifically for you. You will discover and hear what is right for you. I encourage you to do your own research for inspiration to find some words of wisdom which resonate for you. There is space below for you to record anything that you liked and you would like to remember in particular.

Exercise: *Notes on Wise Words on Love and Loving Action of Others*

Examples of Reverence That Resonate With me.

Learning how to love others and ourselves, however we learn it, is wonderful, and putting it into practice is even better!

SECTION 3

Living and Becoming Love™

'You can change the world through love with small acts of kindness and compassion, like a smile or a helping hand; you can do it in your own way. Whatever your way is, however you can and in whatever way feels right for you, change the world with love!'

Nicola van Dyke

CHAPTER 7

Becoming Love™ in Practice

Collaboration

We are a team! We are all humans. If we all pull together the possibilities are endless. We can change the planet!

Once, a long time ago, a fellow mentor got cross with me because she felt I was encroaching on her 'patch'. We lived in the same city, which is a big city with an international airport. She wrote me a rather unpleasant email saying that my prices were too low, even though I was using the industry guidelines, and that I didn't understand that our industry was all about abundance. She was right I didn't have this understanding. I neither linked the idea of abundance solely to finance, nor felt that my motivation for being a mentor was solely my own financial abundance. I was a relatively new mentor having changed career within the last few years, and gave her words a lot of thought. I didn't want to fall out with her or anyone and I didn't want there to be a feeling of unpleasantness between us or any of the other healers and mentors in our city. So, I thought about it some more and emailed her back, thanking her for her insight and advice. I told her that she was right. I didn't 'understand' that my work was all about abundance. I understood that for me, it was all about love. I didn't ignore her or confront her. I didn't feel anger or hurt. I listened to what she thought and respected her beliefs but was assertive and kind in my response. I'm sure we still hold very different beliefs about many things now, all these years later, but she is a very smart, successful lady and I have utmost respect for her.

None of us operate in a vacuum and we must accept that by our uniqueness, we all have different belief systems. None of us are right all the time or wrong all the time. It is possible to be true to your authentic self without being confrontational with others, or feeling victimised. You can be in your own power whilst accepting others have their own power. You neither have to agree with the other person all the time nor let them be in control of your decisions.

> *'Here I stand. I see you. I see where*
> *you stand and I love you.'*
> Nicola van Dyke

Abundance is wonderful, don't get me wrong, I am all for it! Abundance of everything: health; friends; fun; money; success, wonder and love. Manifesting our lives and co-creating what we want in our life is a wonderful tool! We hear all the time on social media, the internet, in motivational books and speeches, that it is possible to co-create our lives. I am a great believer in this. I call it *manifesting,* however these techniques can be used for so much more than a new car or one hundred students whose tickets will pay your bills. It is understood within these ideologies that you cannot manifest for anyone else as each person has their own free will. That is true, I think, but you can manifest for *you* to be in a position to love, support and help others if you choose to and they accept it.

Near the beginning of this book I introduced you to my 'God Dream'. I dream of something profound and amazing. I dream of being able to feel reverence in its purest form, and then shine the feeling out to such an extent that it radiates out of me and reaches others. I imagine this loving feeling is then absorbed by each person that I meet until they feel completely loved and able to revere others. Once full of love, my dream is that each of these people then shine and radiate out reverence to others. Through this chain reaction, eventually every human in the world is in a happy, healthy state of love. It is an amazing thought. It's a dream - but I'm working on it!

Just imagine if you or I could manifest that kind of change in the world. If we could, then manifesting a new house or a new car would be easy. Those kind of day to day 'human' items which seem so important to us would be no problem at all to co-create. With this in mind, my advice to you is to have a 'God Dream', one where money is no object. A dream that is so big that it seems far out of the realms of human possibly. If you have huge dreams, that seem almost impossible and completely out of your day to day experience, then the simple things will fall into place with more ease. There is a well-known expression that if you shoot for the moon and end up just as far as the stars, then that is a pretty good place to be!

There is space below to write about your 'God Dream'. Think big! This is the dream that no money could buy in its entirety. It often takes a while to get into this mode of thinking. You need to get your head past the fleet of new cars or the private tropical island! Just let your imagination go and remember there is no one dream better than another. We are all allowed to have whatever dream we choose without feeling selfish or stupid. What is your 'God Dream'?

My God Dream....

Having a 'God dream' benefits you personally, but imagine what could happen if we all collaborate in this request for love into our amazing universe. Just imagine how we can change the planet through our ability to love. You guys are awesome, we are an amazing network of humanity and we can do anything if we work together! People all over the world rely and believe in the power of prayer and how that power is magnified when more people share the same wish. The combined force of humans is not just limited to prayer either. Every day all over the world, people gather in groups to support changes to the law of their country, to demonstrate, to hold vigils or to add their name to a protest. There is evidence that the hole in the ozone layer is now shrinking (*National Geographic, Aaron Sidder June 2016*). Scientists such as Susan Solomon put it down to the world cutting down on the use of CFC gases such as the use of aerosols.

> *'It is opening later, it is smaller, and its depth is depleted. All of the measurements are independent, and when they all point to this [healing], it is hard to imagine any other explanation.'*
>
> Susan Solomon

I love that she uses the word *healing* in her explanation. She says the hole in the ozone layer is *healing*. Surely our combined use of less CFC gases is key, but what about the power of the human collective consciousness changing? Did the outcry, the demonstrations, the prayers and the love we as human beings sent to the environment also help? I love to think so! I really believe that we can do anything as a beautiful team of humanity if we set our minds to it and work with love.

If we use our energy to squabble and to compete negatively, comparing ourselves unfavourably with each other instead of concentrating on the best we can be, are we wasting our skills and gifts, as well as our time? If it is true that we each came here with a purpose, I'm pretty sure that none of your purposes involved fighting with others. As a team of humans, a wonderful network of humanity, we can move forward with love and do wonderful things. We can move forward as individuals when we clear up our own negativity, and we can move forward as a team when we work on our jealousy and fear of each other.

It is widely thought that an element of competition can be healthy and I think we should be in competition with ourselves to be the best we can be. In our jobs and personal life, we can aim to give of our best, in the time we have. We can aim to teach our children, to pass on positive learning with respect, to ensure they are empowered to be wonderful human beings. This type of competition with yourself is coming from love and is a win/win situation. We cannot all come first in the 100-metre dash at school, but we can all choose to compete. Few gold medallists will say that all the joy is in the first-place award. That may be the goal and the 'cherry on the cake', but the joy is in the whole experience of being the best you can be. Sportsmen and women want to win but they have utmost respect for their fellow competitors and their journeys. They recognise that they all have common interests and goals, common struggles and joys. They know that the act of training and competing is the common joy they share.

I remember my youngest daughter at the age of four being absolutely thrilled after running in a race at her nursery school and being given a star shaped sticker as she crossed the finish line. She ran up to me with a big smile on her face telling me she had won. Her friend who actually crossed the finish line first, looked at her aghast and told her in no uncertain terms that *she* had won and that my daughter didn't understand what winning was. My daughter gave her a big hug and said, *'I know what winning is, silly. This was so much fun. We all won, and you ran the fastest, well done!'* To really win in life you can win, and allow others to also win from their perspective. Life can be a 'win win' situation for all if we each show reverence for ourselves, for our family, love for the human race and the planet.

How to Recognise What is Yours and What is Others' 'Stuff'!

I believe that the essence of loving others is to empower others, not to have them dependent on us. Whatever you are experiencing in your journey and in your life now, keep your vibration high, treat others with reverence and let your authentic self shine out. Love people. Love begets love. Be an example and keep shining. Their journey is theirs. Yours is yours.

> *'The greatest thing that you can do in life is to live to your peak and to set an example that there is a way to live beyond all limitations.'*
> Sadhguru

The universe is like a mirror, it reflects back our thoughts and actions. If you think you are disliked, you will look for signs to prove yourself right, because we all want to be right, right? You will notice every time someone says anything that could be slightly unkind or derogatory and you will twist it subconsciously in your mind so it appears as more evidence that you are disliked. Sometimes when we hold negative belief programmes we are unable to see when others are being genuine, being kind or coming from love.

If we are filled with anger, resentment or self-criticism, then we may react to others' words and actions in a way that creates unnecessary conflict. Let me give you an example: A few years ago, when my son was only 5, myself and a friend were out walking in a large park with our little boys. The children were playing a chasing game around an ornamental pond which had stone carvings of animals at each corner. My son shouted to his friend that they should run separate ways and meet at the big, fat elephant at the far corner. His friend's mother was standing near that corner and reacted with hurt and pain. She shouted at him that he was a horrible, nasty boy to call her such disgusting names. She was angry that he had been so rude. She told him it was very unkind to refer to her as an 'elephant' and that people's weight was not something to ridicule. She was very upset. He was shocked and confused. He had been talking about the stone carving of the elephant. She had not even noticed it, as she was so caught up in her own feelings of self-criticism. Even when he pointed it out, she was not convinced. Her belief systems prevented her from seeing and hearing the truth.

The more we 'clear up our stuff', the more we see the truth, and the more we *can* see the truth. The more we can Become Love. Changing our negative beliefs to positive ones may not necessarily change others but it will change the way you internalise information and react to others.

Are you ready to clear up some of your 'stuff'? Below are some beliefs or programmes that you may have which could be holding you back from finding the ability to collaborate and interact with others in your life. In the first chapter of this book, you will find some information on how to test for beliefs that you may consciously or subconsciously hold. Test the beliefs below now, to see if you have any of these programmes. Remember, just because you test 'Yes' or 'No' to any of these beliefs, it doesn't mean it is true. It just means on some level *you* believe it is true. So, if you lean forward when testing belief 10, *'Others hate me,'* that doesn't mean that they do. It just means on some conscious or unconscious level, you feel or believe they do. When testing yourself, if you do have any of the limiting beliefs, you can just put a pen mark next to them. If you have the 'desired response,' do not mark them at all; they do not apply to you and you don't have to think about them.

Stand up and test the beliefs below now, as described how to in Chapter 1. Remember to ensure that you are testing YES/NO correctly before you start, to speak aloud and to have your eyes closed.

Exercise: *Belief Programmes Regarding Enjoying Being with Others, to Check For:*

	Belief to Check	Desired Response	Your check mark*
1	There is always enough for me	Yes	
2	There is enough financial abundance in the universe.	Yes	
3	There is enough financial abundance for me.	Yes	
4	I am recognised and respected by others.	Yes	
	I am recognised and respected by my family.	Yes	
	I am recognised and respected by friends.	Yes	
	I am recognised and respected by colleagues	Yes	
	I am recognised and respected by Creator. (Use any word that works for you here)	Yes	
	I am recognised and respected by -------. (Name someone here if you wish to)	Yes	

5	I am valued by others.	Yes	
	I am valued by my family.	Yes	
	I am valued by my friends.	Yes	
	I am valued by colleagues.	Yes	
	I am valued by Creator. (Use any word that works for you here)	Yes	
	I am valued by -------------- (Name someone here if you wish to).	Yes	
6	I can work in a team without fear.	Yes	
7	I can work in a team without jealousy.	Yes	
8	I am alone.	No	
9	I have to work alone.	No	
10	Others hate me.	No	
	Others fear me.	No	
	Others scare me.	No	
	Others are jealous of me.	No	
11	Other people dislike me.	No	
	Other people disregard me.	No	
12	I am important.	Yes	
13	I am special.	Yes	

If you do hold any of these potentially limiting beliefs programmes, and you will probably hold many of them, don't panic! By the time you have read this book, practised the exercises and listened to the meditations, you will already be much closer to Becoming Love™ and you will have already changed many of these beliefs within you. We are all learning all the time through increased self-recognition and practising Becoming Love™. Come back to them at the end, re-test the ones you thought you held and enjoy witnessing the transformation. (You do not need to test those you never held in the first place, just the ones you originally marked.) If, after this, you find you are still holding some of these beliefs or if you would like to clear them faster, there are different ways of doing this and these are discussed in chapter 1. Do not worry if you feel you hold many of these programmes now; you are a beautiful work in progress and already perfect.

Being Motivated by Love for Humanity

What drives you? What are you motivated by? The next section takes a look at how this can affect your ability to love humanity. Becoming Love™ is easy if you are motivated by it, if love for others is one of your motivations. Of course, we all need to pay our bills but if money is our only motivation than that would imply, if we were wealthy enough, we would stop doing whatever it is we are doing. If all of us who earn our living by supporting others suddenly became so financially abundant that we just stopped doing it, many people would be negatively affected. Just take a moment to think about all the professions which support and help others on a day to day basis:

- *Drivers of buses, taxis, coaches, trains and trams*

- *Hairdressers, manicurists, personal shoppers, and beauticians*

- *Doctors, nurses, dentists, surgeons, therapists and healers*

- *Teachers, classroom assistants, caretakers and cleaners*

- *Chefs, waiters, concierges and receptionists*

- *Care workers, mechanics, plumbers, pizza deliverers and personal trainers*

These lists could go on and on! You may not even recognise that the work you do supports others at all, but actually most of us in some way or another support other humans in some way. It may be that you work in an industry traditionally associated with helping others such as the medical profession. Or it could be that in the course of your everyday job you are supporting others with love without realising it. Most of us interact with others as part of our work, and have several opportunities within the day to show reverence for those people and to make a difference to them in the moment. You can choose to smile and be kind in all that you do. You can have a friendly conversation and you can choose to interact and act with integrity. We all can, and every time we do so, we can make a small positive difference to someone else.

If you had all the money in the world, would you just stop working and interacting with so many people and sit by a pool somewhere exotic? If you had several houses and cars and lots of money in the bank, would you still work? If you did step back from your busy work life, maybe less people would benefit from your love. If our purpose is to support others and we are motivated by money, maybe on a subconscious level we only earn just what we need but no more. This ensures we continue to carry on supporting and showing love for others in our day to day working life.

So how about letting the universe take care of the money, trusting it to see your wishes and desires through your actions and behaviour, so that you can have other motivations? You can be motivated by being the best you can be at what you do. You could be motivated by your 'God Dream', whatever that is for you. How about being motivated by love for others or by love for humanity? Trust that all you need in terms of abundance is there. Have confidence in yourself to know that there is always enough. Could you be motivated by helping the world or by being reverent? If you can make these your motivations you will be an unstoppable force of love. That doesn't mean you stop taking action towards financial abundance, it just means you become aware of other motivations in your life.

I am motivated by my 'God Dream' and by what I feel is my life's purpose. I am motivated by my wish to learn about love and share that with others; by having reverence for others. I trust the universe to take care of the abundance and have changed my belief systems to find motivation in love. It is so much easier to love others when love is one of your motivations!

CHAPTER 8

Living and Becoming Love™

Having worked through this book, and enjoyed the meditations, you are closer and closer to Becoming Love™, but you need to go out there and live it, be it and do it.

Be Kind

Listen to people. Be in the moment with yourself and others. See them as they truly are and love them anyway. Speak and act from love. Smiling at people and acting with kindness are ways to show love for humanity. 'The universe is set up for spirals' (Vianna Stibal, July 2015), so the more you smile and act kindly, the more people will reflect it back to you and others. You can spread love through a community in a morning by smiling at one person as you pas them on the street. You don't have to know someone to see their heart or their soul. You don't have to know them to love them.

Gratitude

Show gratitude to those you meet and to yourself. Feeling grateful has an amazing effect on our own well-being as well as what happens around us. Saying 'thank you' and feeling it, to others, to yourself, and to the universe, makes us feel content and bountiful. Further, those of you already versed in the concept of the Law of Attraction will recognise that the more we act as if we have what it is we seek, the sooner we attract it. Gratitude is the icing on the cake - the more we are grateful for what we already have, the more we attract similar things to us.

Are you grateful for the loved ones in your life? Do you show and tell them how much you value their support, love and friendship? Finding some loving aspect of your life, however small, to be grateful for every day, is a positive step toward Becoming Love™. Some people like to make a written note of one thing that has bought love into their life or reminded them about love, to be grateful for, every day or every week. They keep a gratitude journal or make little notes on small pieces of paper and put them into a 'gratitude jar'. Keeping these notes adds to the joy of Becoming Love™ and can become a great focal point for you when you are feeling low.

Exercise: *Expressing Gratitude*

As a start, why not take thirty days to try it out? For the next month, take the time to notice at least one aspect of love every day that you feel grateful for. It can be anything from something you feel privileged to have seen, a relationship you have, how the sunshine lifted your mood, or how your fitness class boosted your confidence…something, different every day. There is space to write down thirty days' worth below; but don't let that limit you! Once you begin to feel the value of this practice you can continue it as long as you like!

Day	Today I am grateful for….
1	
2	
3	
4	
5	
6	
7	
8	
9	
10	
11	
12	
13	
14	
15	

Nicola van Dyke

Day	Today I am grateful for….
16	
17	
18	
19	
20	
21	
22	
23	
24	
25	
26	
27	
28	
29	
30	

Clear up your stuff!

How can you expect the world to love you, if you don't love yourself? How can you expect others to love you, if you don't love them? Do you hate your friend because last month she met a new boyfriend and now she has stopped hanging out with you so much? Do you hate your colleague who presented your idea as their own to your boss? Work through the scenario in your mind objectively, see them and the situation from the highest perspective. Practise forgiveness. You don't have to like everyone or choose to hang out with them, but you can love them.

This exercise is designed to assist you in acquiring certain feelings which will help you to Become Love and practise it in your day to day life. Firstly, take a pen and read the statements of feelings below. Circle YES to any of them that you would like to feel or think you already do feel. The second part of this exercise is to make yourself comfortable and listen to the *track 10,* on the **Becoming Love™ Meditation Album**. All of these feelings below are included on *track 10,* **Becoming Love™** *Every Day Meditation* which you can listen to and enjoy now, later and as many times as you like.

Exercise: *Becoming Love™ Every Day!*

Feelings You Already Have or Would Like to Have	Circle the word YES if you would like to have this feeling or feel you already do have it.
Would you like to already know how to and what it feels like to Become Love?	YES
Would you like to already know how to and what it feels like to practise love for humanity?	YES
Would you like to know that is possible for you to Become Love?	YES
Would you like to know that you are worthy and deserving of Becoming Love™?	YES
Would you like know that it is safe for you to do so?	YES
Would you like to know how to Become Love without being overwhelmed or having to take on others' emotions and pain?	YES
Would you like to already know how to and what it feels like to act with reverence?	YES
Would you like to already know how to and what it feels like to revere others with love from the highest perspective?	YES
Would you like to already know how to and what it feels like to touch others with reverence?	YES
Would you like to already know how to and what it feels like to see others with reverence?	YES

Would you like to already know how to and what it feels like to touch others with reverence?	YES
Would you like to already know how to and what it feels like to listen to others with reverence?	YES
Would you like to already know how to and what it feels like to speak to others with reverence?	YES
Would you like to already know how to and what it feels like to work with others with reverence?	YES
Would you like to already know how to and what it feels like to communicate with others with reverence?	YES
Would you like to already know how to and what it feels like to behave towards others with reverence?	YES
Would you like to already know how to and what it feels like to know others with reverence?	YES
Would you like to already know how to and what it feels like to know how to and what it feels like to understand others with reverence?	YES
Would you like to already know how to and what it feels like to love yourself with reverence?	YES
Would you like to already know how to and what it feels like to revere yourself?	YES
Would you like to already know how to and what it feels like to revere Creator/ the highest energy/the universe? *	YES
*(substitute whatever word works for you here)	

Meditation: *Becoming Love™ Everyday*

Make yourself comfortable in a quiet place where you will not be disturbed for about 30 minutes. You could sit or lie down. Now, listen to the **Becoming Love™ Everyday Meditation** which is *track 10*, on the **Becoming Love™ Meditation Album.**

All of the feelings in the exercise above are included on this meditation; as you listen to it, you can just allow the sound of my voice to wash over you and relax. You don't need to respond if you hear me asking you a question because by completing the questions above you have already made your intentions clear, but if you choose to affirm or not in your head, you can do so.

If you find you lose track of what I am saying, don't worry, just allow yourself to sense whatever comes to you.

Relax and enjoy now!

CHAPTER 9

How Do You Know When You Are Becoming Love™?

Exercise: *How Will I Feel When I am Becoming Love ™?*

What do you think? How do you think you will know? How do you think you will feel when you feel more self-love and love for others? There is some space to write your thoughts below.

When I am Becoming Love™, I will feel….

In my experience, the more you love yourself and you love others, the more these wonderful changes start to happen:

- The more you love, the happier you will feel. There is a sense of detachment, of seeing humanity from afar. It is not that you don't care, it is more that you see, but you do not get drawn into the drama or feel negative emotions.

- You see beauty and wonder everywhere in the universe; in every flower, every sunset and all around you everywhere you go. You start to notice this beautiful planet in all its intricate splendour.

- You see acts of human kindness and of love everywhere you look. Small random acts of kindness and love by people living their lives. There is a bus driver on one of my local routes who stops the bus, gets out, rings on the front door bell and assists an elderly lady out of her house onto the bus, if she is not waiting at the bus stop. My family have witnessed this a couple of times and remarked on his kindness and servitude. You will notice people helping others in small ways every day because you are attuned with love.

- You will be able to see and define a person's unhappiness, discomfort or anger in a moment and, with your own reaction, response and attitude, be able flip them back into love. You can diffuse dramas and conflicts with the way you react to people and what they say to you. Your kindness will warm them because they will know they are loved.

- People will start to look at you because you shine. Babies, children and animals will actually look right at you because they see love. (On a precautionary note you may find that people mistake what they feel for you as romantic love, so you may need to be more aware of your own body language so that you are projecting agape rather than romantic love, except to those you choose to.)

- Where ever you go, people are nice to you. You start to notice this and so do others. I used to point out to my children and friends how nice people are: at the airport; at the garage; at the market and in town. One day one of my daughters exclaimed that of course they are. 'Everyone is always nice to you, Mummy. Haven't you noticed?' You will know if you are slipping out of the energy of agape as people will react differently to you, so you can adjust yourself, work out what has happened to change you and get back on track.

- You will find you are more at one with yourself. You will become more in touch with your own physical, emotional and spiritual needs.

When you are Becoming Love™, you are more in alignment with the universe and it works with you to make your life easier. Whether you believe it is fate, any number of coincidences, just luck or down to a significant unknown series of events, in my experience, the more you Become Love, the more the universe appears to reflect your wishes and desires. It happens to me every day in small ways, and some days in big ways. Free upgrades on air travel, people coming into my life to support me just when I need them, ideas which come out of nowhere and getting a parking space right outside my apartment when it is tipping down with rain! The term I use is manifesting and there is lots more I could tell you about this but suffice to say, the more you Become Love, the easier it is to create your life. The following example is one of my more spectacular and mysterious successes.

A year or so ago, I was waiting for a train to take me to London where I was due to teach a week-long seminar. It was a bitterly cold, dark evening in November and driving, icy rain was lashing down, blown across the platform by the freezing wind. My mother and my youngest daughter were waiting with me. My daughter was due to be staying with my mother whilst I was away and had insisted that they come to see me off on the platform. As we got onto the correct concourse, the station announcement said the train was delayed for at least half an hour and possibly longer. As we looked around at all the other despondent passengers waiting, all of a sudden, the electronic notices started to spell out there was now an indefinite delay on the London train's arrival. Then seconds later it announced that the train was cancelled. Some passengers began to shuffle off the platform to find out when the next one would be arriving, if at all that night. It was dark and we were very cold. My daughter was getting anxious and upset at the thought of our week's separation which she found very difficult. My mother was getting impatient as she just wanted to go home into the warm, and found my daughter's concerns a little over dramatic. I knew once I had left it would be easier for them both and I didn't want to get to London too late as I was teaching the next day. I had these thoughts in a second and I felt love and empathy for both my mother and my daughter. A minute or so later a train drew into the station. All the people waiting looked at each other, and then around the platform. There was no electronic announcement and the train had no signage. There was nobody visible on the train and all the passengers on the platform were unsure what was going on. After a minute or two, a station guard came puffing up the slope to the platform waving his arms around and telling us all that this was the London train and we should all get on it if we wanted to get to London that night. For no reason and without warning, it had arrived, only a couple of minutes late. The electronic notices still said it was cancelled, and when I asked him, the station guard had no idea why it had suddenly arrived or where exactly it had come from.... But it had come and it was going to London. Love brought it! I kissed and hugged my family and hopped on thanking the universe!

Becoming love™ will change your ability to create your life whether you are initially aware of it or not. From the smile of a stranger to any number of amazing possibilities out there for you, as you Become Love, it will change your life and the lives of everyone you meet. Be that smiling stranger and change someone else's day!

CHAPTER 10

Are you ready?

You can now go out and be love, love others and make a difference to the planet in whatever way is right for you. You are awesome! I love the idea of all of us wonderful human beings working together to raise the vibration of the planet with love.

I invite you to be a radiator not a drain!

You are constantly being invited to show your love for humanity and, if you align yourself with love, then every meeting, every relationship with another, however brief, will be one of love. An inability to do this is sometimes down to your fears, but fear is not so much a 'thing' but a lack of something. Fear is a lack of love. Don't keep checking in with your mobile phone, check in with the energy of love deep within you! Ask yourself what would love do?

You can make small differences every day just by smiling at a person when you walk past them. You don't need their permission, you are coming from love. You can go out and feel people's hearts and souls, and in doing so love them. You can choose to start or continue a huge project which spreads love to the world. You can offer your services voluntarily to a neighbour, a local charity or your community. You can choose to show love and kindness though your words, your eyes and your smile, as you go about your day. You can Become Love in your own way. You are unique and all of us can change the planet in our own way, big or small, every day. Whether you are a barrister or a book shop owner, a hairdresser or a homemaker, a therapist or a taxi driver, we all can show love for each other in our own way.

'Let me love you better!' This is a phrase used in Britain by a parent or carer to a child when they fall over or are hurt. They gather the tearful child up into a hug and 'love them better.' Let me love *you* better. Let us love each other better. Let us love humanity better. Let us love the world better!

Don't be discouraged if people don't notice your efforts. For some, who are not as fortunate as you, those who are full of fears, resentments, anger and hatred, they genuinely cannot recognise that you are coming from love. There is an old saying that 'Good can see evil, but evil cannot see good.' I am not suggesting or saying that anyone is evil; I genuinely don't believe that to be true. However, if someone has not been loved, seen love or felt love, then it may take them a while to recognise it, but your continuing shining and patience will be stronger than any negativity. Love is the strongest energy in the universe.

There is nothing new in this message. For thousands of years people have been saying that we should love one another, how to do it, why it is important and encouraging others to do so. In the past, humans working together with love have made worldwide changes. Slavery was considered normal in many parts of the world for centuries. People were taken from their homelands, shipped in horrific conditions for thousands of miles and forced to work without a choice. This was considered the right of the captors, as if the people they had enslaved had no rights or freedom of choice. This accepted way of life stopped as an accepted practice, because people stood up for the love of humanity and spoke up. Not just one, but many all over the world, and some of those people were in positions of enough power to make a difference and in other cases it was the voices of many who were heard.

Some of these slave ships stopped en- route from Africa to America, in a port in England called Liverpool, north of the little country, Wales. The copper industry in Wales was largely supported by the slave trade industry because the copper and brass were used to make goods the slave traders could barter with. In Cuba, wealthy Welsh mine owners found high grade copper and rented slaves from the Spanish to work the mine even into the 1860s, well after slavery was abolished in the UK. My 3x great grandfather was Welsh. He was alive in the early 1800s when the slave trade ships were still common. He was not rich or well educated but he spoke up. He spoke at chapel about loving humanity. In the Methodist church or chapel, anyone can stand and talk or preach to the congregation if they wish to. He travelled around South Wales and preached in small village chapels that it was wrong to take a man from his home and family against his will and to force him to work in terrible conditions. He preached about equality of men and about recognising all men as equal human beings regardless of their skin colour, language or culture. He encouraged others to see that we are all humans and equal in God's eyes. He was just one of many hundreds and thousands of people who through love, changed the world as it was.

We can change the world through love. You can change the world through love – in small acts of kindness and compassion, like a smile or a helping hand; you can do it in your own way. Working as a network of humanity in the past, we humans have made wonderful changes to the world. Whatever your way is, however you can and in whatever way feels right for you, change the world with love. Let's continue! Let's do it now! Let's make a difference together, by holding hands across the world and Becoming Love™!

Meditation: *Becoming Love*™

> This last meditation on the **Becoming Love™ Meditation Album,** is a gentle way to allow you to express your reverence for humanity. The script for this final meditation is written below so you can come back to it easily any time and read it.
>
> *Breathe in deeply and out, and relax. Feel unconditional love coming through you and within you. Then imagine it shining out of you and spreading out to fill all the people you love dearly in your family and to your friends. Then imagine it shining and spreading out to all the people they love dearly. To their loved ones, and to their loved one's loved ones…and their loved ones' loved ones. Then imagine it filling all the people in the world today who are in pain, who are scared, who are lonely and who are caring for others. Imagine the love spreading to every single human on this planet so we are all filled with unconditional love; a network of humanity connected by love. Breathe in, breathe out and open your eyes.*
>
> If you find you lose track of what I am saying, don't worry, just allow yourself to sense whatever comes to you. Just allow the feeling of love, reverence and compassion for others to flow through you and around you.
>
> Make yourself comfortable in a quiet place where you will not be disturbed for about 20 minutes. You could sit or lie down. Now, listen to the *Becoming Love Meditation* which is *track 11,* on the **Becoming Love™ Meditation Album.**
>
> Relax and enjoy now!

Nicola van Dyke

Thank you for reading this book.

Thank you for the love you bring to the world.

I stand here. I see you. I see where you stand and I love you.

USEFUL INFORMATION

Download the Becoming Love™ Meditation Album

1. Online, visit the website www.nicolavandyke.com
2. Follow the instructions from the home page to the Becoming Love ™ album download page.
3. Follow the instructions to input your email and the following download code: **MY25364957-3645**
4. You can then use the album which has been downloaded to your device.

The album is also available to listen to on Soundcloud via the link: https://soundcloud.com/user-530532855/sets/becoming-love-meditation-1/s-rJ7Jp

Relevant Websites

Author website: www.nicolavandyke.com
Official ThetaHealing® website: www.thetahealing.com
Bruce Lipton: www.brucelipton.com
Book Cover Artist, Nancy Green, website: www.artintheta.com

ABOUT THE AUTHOR

Nicola van Dyke is a world renown life coach & mentor who specialises in making positive changes to people's lives. She has a global client base and travels extensively teaching seminars and workshops. Her bi-weekly radio show also called Becoming Love™, encompasses her ideology and through discussions, live healing sessions and guided meditations, inspires and encourages a global audience.

Recognised as the Healer for the healers, she is passionate about showing people how to love each other, themselves, their life and this beautiful universe we exist within. She is committed to assisting people in becoming their authentic selves, and co-creating the life they wish for and deserve. She guides people on a journey of self-acceptance and self-wisdom through her mentoring programmes.

Her educational background includes a First class degree (BSc Hons) from the University of Aston and a Post Graduate degree in Education with distinction from Southampton University. She has a Diploma in Life Coaching with distinction and is a Master ThetaHealing® Instructor, with a certification of Science. She lives in Edinburgh, UK with her children.

Printed in Poland
by Amazon Fulfillment
Poland Sp. z o.o., Wrocław

53047695R00114